Dedication

*This devotional is dedicated to
my children, Janae and Jadon. Both of you (along with
your father) are God's best gifts to me. May your hearts be
encouraged with these personal reflections, may you receive
a revelation from God concerning your divine greatness,
giftedness, value and purpose, may you gain God's
perspective on all of your life situations and may God, who
has appointed you for His good purpose, grant you success
all the days of your life.*

*Remember. God is able to do immeasurably more than
you could ever ask or imagine. Your best is yet to come
so keep trusting God and believing Him for life MORE
abundantly! I love you to infinity and beyond!*

Contents

Section 1

YOUR PURPOSE

Section 2

YOUR PERSPECTIVE

Section 3

Section 4

Devotional Overview

SECTION 1: Your Purpose

In this section, you'll discover what you were made for. You'll also explore your divine design—how you were shaped for your purpose. The goal of this section is to help you understand why you were deliberately created and how you were strategically formed for a specific purpose. This understanding will prevent you from settling for less, forfeiting your divine assignments, or delaying your destiny.

SECTION 2: Your Perspective

In this section, you'll learn to view your disappointments as divine appointments, your unplanned paths as divine redirections, and your setbacks as divine setups. You'll also discover how to replace positive self-talk with faith-based talk. The goal of this section is to help you cultivate the mind of Christ in all life situations so you can receive a revelation of God's plan and purpose for your life.

SECTION 3: Your Value

In this section, you will uncover how God has divinely designed and equipped you to be His ambassador. You'll also learn how to assess your worth, take control of negative self-narratives, and embrace God's story regarding your identity and value. The goal of this section is to help you understand who and what defines your worth so that you won't strive for, long for, or live for the approval, validation, or recognition of others.

SECTION 4: Your Success

This section focuses on biblical principles for achieving godly success. The goal is to guide you in finding favor and success in the eyes of God, ensuring that you won't be deceived by one of Satan's greatest tools: counterfeit success.

Self-Reflection and Prayer Guide

Each devotional concludes with *Reflection* questions to help you journal your thoughts and consider how to apply biblical principles to your life. A *Remember* statement reinforces a key point from the devotional, and a *Resolve* statement helps you commit to a specific course of action.

A written *Prayer* is also included to guide your conversation with God on each topic. As you reflect on your personal experiences and ask God to show you how to apply new insights to your life, you will create space for Him to transform you from the inside out.

Whether you are seeking to discover your God-given purpose and value, looking for a fresh perspective to guide you through life's challenges and disappointments, or striving to understand how to achieve success God's way, this book was written for you. If you commit to meditating on God's Word daily and obeying His teachings, God will do His part to make you fruitful and successful all the days of your life.

INTRODUCTION

A life without a clear sense of purpose
feels meaningless, aimless and directionless.
But knowing your divine purpose creates vision.
And vision leads to your God-given mission.

Without knowing God's vision for your life,
you drift to undesired destinations
because His vision is a compass that sets your life direction
and fuels your divine purpose.

When you understand your divine purpose
it changes your goals and social circles.
Your God-given purpose directs your focus, efforts and priorities.
It shapes your perspective and sparks joy in your heart.
It guides your thoughts, decisions and actions.
Purpose doesn't make life easy. It makes it meaning-full.

Did you know the source of your purpose is in the mind of your Creator?
Purpose is the reason why you exist and it is only given to you by God.
When you discover and obey God's purpose for your life,
you are truly successful because success is measured by
your obedience and living out your God-given purpose.

Purpose is doing not only doing GOOD things,
it's doing the RIGHT things.
And YOUR 'right things' must be disclosed to you by God.
Just know that when you seek God 's presence over your purpose
His divine purpose will surely find you.

Radhika Cruz

Your Purpose

YOU WERE CREATED ON PURPOSE TO FULFILL GOD'S PURPOSES.

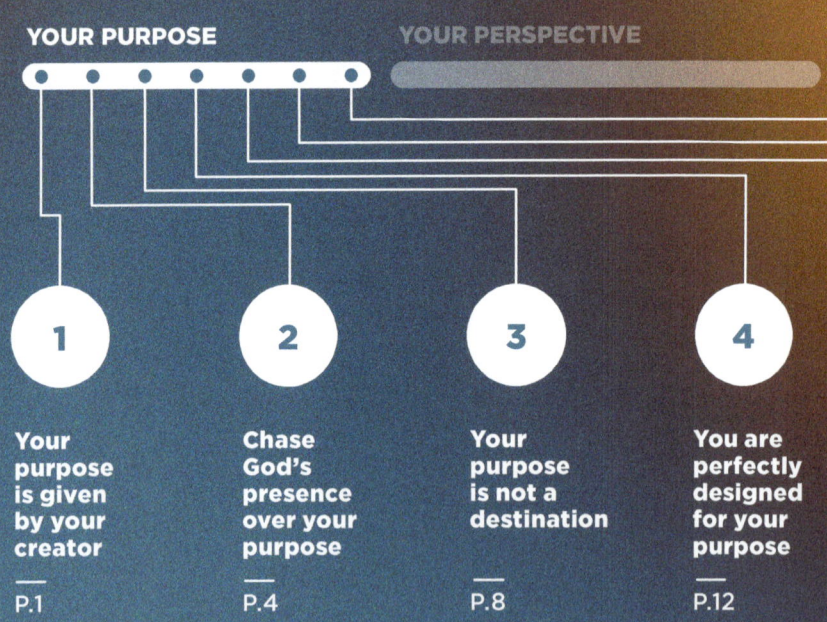

YOUR PURPOSE

YOUR PERSPECTIVE

1

Your purpose is given by your creator

2

Chase God's presence over your purpose

3

Your purpose is not a destination

4

You are perfectly designed for your purpose

"When you chase God's presence, His purpose will find you."

Radhika Cruz

1

Your purpose is given by your Creator

Before I shaped you in the womb, I knew all about you.
Before you saw the light of day, I had holy plans for you.
JEREMIAH 1:5 MSG

D
ISCOVERING AND FULFILLING ONE'S PURPOSE IS A HOT TOPIC today. Everywhere you look, there's a book, advertisement, sermon, or podcast on how to discover your purpose. This is such a popular subject because, without a sense of purpose, life often feels meaningless, aimless, and, some might say, even pointless.

Knowing why you were created is not only essential for your psychological well-being but also critical for your spiritual well-being. Pastor Rick Warren says, "If you didn't create yourself, you can't discover the meaning and purpose for your life by yourself." We cannot discover our God-given purpose apart from knowing the One who created us for His own purposes. Your purpose is found in the mind of your Creator, and knowing why you were created cannot be discovered apart from knowing the One who made you. To discover your purpose is to first discover your Creator—only He can reveal His purpose for you, His masterpiece.

When you uncover God's purpose for your life, it should directly shape what you do with it. A great example of this is seen in the life of Jeremiah, where God said, *"Before I shaped you in the womb, I knew all about you. Before you saw the light of day, I had holy plans for you: a prophet to the nations—that's what I had in mind for you"* (Jeremiah 1:5).

God has a holy purpose in mind for you.

Here, God reveals Jeremiah's purpose: to be His prophet to the nations. Once Jeremiah understood God's purpose for his life, he knew what he was meant to do. Knowing he was created to be a prophet, he recognized he had to function as one because **purpose** (or form) **dictates function**.

Just as God had a holy purpose for Jeremiah, He has a holy purpose for you. But to discover what He has in mind for you, you must seek Him first (Matthew 6:33). *It's up to you to not only uncover and understand God's purpose, but also up to you to live it out.*

As I explored God's Word concerning the primary purpose we've been created for, here's what I discovered. We are God's *workmanship*, His *masterpiece*, created in Christ Jesus to do good works He prepared in advance for us to do. (Ephesians 2:10). We are also God's royal priesthood, His special possession and because of that, we are to proclaim His goodness to the world. (1 Peter 2:9).

Additionally, we are Christ's ambassadors, His chosen ones appointed to share the good news message of reconciliation and salvation through Him (2 Corinthians 5:18-20). I discovered we were created to reconcile unbelievers to God because He's not willing that any should perish but all come to repentance (2 Peter 3:9). Furthermore, we've been commissioned as Christ's witnesses to go into all the world and make disciples, training others to follow His teachings. (Matthew 28:19). Therefore, we are disciple-makers who are to share the reason for the hope we have (1 Peter 3:15). Your spiritual purpose is very clear. It's not too late for you to embrace God's purpose for your life so you can begin aligning your actions to what He has created you to do. All you have to do is obey. **Remember, because you're not dead, God's not done.** He has so much MORE in store for you; a life and legacy of abundance!

RETHINK:
What do I need to rethink when it comes to my spiritual purpose?

_____
_____
_____
_____
_____
_____

REFLECT:
What has God created me to do according to His word? What action do I need to take to ensure I'm living out God's vision and purpose for my life?

_____
_____
_____
_____
_____
_____

RESOLVE:

I will seek God's face by _____
so I can know and understand His vision and purpose for me.

PRAY:
Father, I recognize my reason for existing can only be discovered in you, my Creator. Help me to remember that your purpose for my life transcends any position, platform, role, or vocation I may have. Father help me to see what you have in mind for me so I can align my will to your purposes. In Jesus' name I pray, amen.

REMEMBER
To discover your divine purpose you must first seek to know the mind of your Creator.

Chase God's presence over your purpose

2

ON MAY 1, 2008, I LOST MY mother to ovarian cancer. She had battled the disease for three years and died a few weeks after her 49th birthday. I remember her saying during her last few weeks of life that she had to get better because she still had a purpose to fulfill on this earth. Hearing these words, I thought:

> "I don't want to arrive at the end of my life believing I have yet to fulfill my God-given purpose. I want to be able to say with confidence that my purpose was fulfilled."

Seek the kingdom of God above all else, and live righteously, and he will give you everything you need.

MATTHEW 6:33 NLT

In complete transparency, though, after my mother's death, a spirit of fear attacked my mind. It told me, *"You are going to die young just like your mother with God's purpose unfulfilled in your life."* I didn't want to admit it, but I had FOMO– the fear of missing out on God's promises and purpose for my life. Fear led me to believe I would die without my purpose being fulfilled, which drove me to 'make moves' I thought would secure *my* destiny.

For example, at 35 years of age, I enrolled in graduate school while raising a twelve-year old and two-year old. I worked full time and volunteered weekly at my local church. I ran myself ragged, trying to be the best student, wife, mother, employee, and volunteer I could be—all so I wouldn't *"miss out"* on fulfilling my purpose on earth. This *'chasing purpose'* caused my heart to be overwhelmed, my body exhausted, and my mind anxious.

My FOMO concerning God's plans and purpose for my life fueled this chase. Fear drove me to strive for more—more accomplishments, more achievements, and more opportunities. Fulfilling my purpose consumed my every thought. Through my own efforts, initiative, and actions, **I was determined to ensure** God's purposes, plans, and promises would be fulfilled in my life. Looking back over my thirties, I now see I was chasing the wrong things. *I was chasing God's purpose for my life rather than chasing God's presence.*

I was striving to **achieve** His promises rather than trusting I would **receive** them. Driven by fear, I doubted God's Word, convinced He might fail me–just as I thought He had failed my mother by not healing her.

Fear led me to question:

Will God really prosper me? Does He really care? Is He truly faithful? I doubted whether God would fulfill His purposes, plans, and promises for my life. I even wondered, God, are you really a GOOD God? Do you truly have good things in store for me?

I wish I could say I immediately recognized the spirit of fear and fought it– but I didn't. Ultimately, I let fear deceive me into believing God couldn't be trusted. I convinced myself God had failed me because He allowed someone I loved to die. It was this significant loss that opened the door for fear to enter my heart. Since I believed God had failed my mom, I thought He would fail me too in delivering on His promise to give me a hope and a prosperous future. This false belief led me to take matters into my own hands, convinced that my future depended on *my own efforts, decisions, initiative, and actions.*

Pictured above and on page 4, SULLIVAN'S ISLAND, SC: *The ocean clears my mind, calms my soul, and reminds me of God's omnipotence.*

With this belief in self-initiative, I reasoned it was up to me to make the necessary calls, plays, and moves to ensure my goals and dreams became my reality. **I thought I was the one** who controlled my destiny. I thought I was *responsible* for ensuring God's purposes would be fulfilled in my life.

Driven by FOMO, I doubted God's goodness, provision, and promise to work out His plans and purpose for my life, and I decided to direct my own path.

But everything changed when I finally got honest with God about my FOMO and disappointment. I remember standing in my bathroom one day, full of anger and disappointment at God because of my mother's death, when I heard God speak to my heart:

"Do you truly trust me with your life and future? Do you really believe I can use your grief and disappointment for good? If you truly trusted me, you would stop striving to get. You would instead be still and receive what I'm giving you. The problem is you don't actually believe I have good things in store for you. And you don't actually believe I will fulfill my plans and promises in your life. Will you stop operating out of fear and truly trust me to fulfill my promises and purposes in your life?"

It was at that moment I decided to live by faith and not by fear. I decided to chase God's presence over His purpose for my life. And I made a decision to stop striving for what I wanted to achieve through my efforts. Instead, I surrendered to what God wanted to give me, recognizing it's His job and not mine, to fulfill His promises and plans for my life.

RETHINK:
What do I need to rethink when it comes to discovering my purpose?

_____

_____

REFLECT:
- How have I been chasing 'purpose' above God's presence?

- What does my striving reveal about my current level of faith and trust in God?

- How can I can better recognize and respond to what God is giving me?

_____

_____

_____

_____

_____

_____

RESOLVE:
I will chase God's presence over my purpose.

PRAY:
Father, I acknowledge that I've been chasing the wrong thing. I've allowed fear to drive my actions rather than my faith. Please forgive me for seeking my purpose over your presence. Help me to confidently trust you'll fulfill your purpose for my life. Help me to stop striving to get, so I can relax and respond to what you're giving. I believe you have good plans for my life. Help me to wait patiently, expectantly and enthusiastically for you to bring your purpose to pass in my life. Thank you for being a good, faithful and loving Father. It's in Jesus' name I ask these things, amen.

REMEMBER
When you seek God first, His purpose will find you.

3 Your purpose is not a destination

F OR SOME REASON, I'VE ALWAYS PERCEIVED PSALM 138:8 AS SPEAKING exclusively of a *future* purpose for my life because the word "WILL" expresses a future tense—something yet to come. But my perspective has since shifted.

For so long, I had fixed my eyes on the future, anticipating what God *will do* —so much so I failed to realize some of His purposes have *already* been fulfilled in my past and some *are being* fulfilled in my life *right now*. What I've come to understand is God's *PURPOSE* for my life is not a destination. It's not a place I reach and then check off a box.

Our God-given purpose is *not limited* to one person, one specific place, one position, one vocation, one location, one mission, one assignment, one time, or one season. Our divine purpose is perpetual and expansive. It is not confined to a single moment in our past, present, or future. It's fluid, multifaceted, multi-layered and multidimensional. It encompasses past, present AND future.

Purpose is what we have already lived. Purpose is what we are living *right now*. And purpose is what *we will live* in the future because our steps and future are ordered by God (Psalms 27:33; Proverbs 19:21).

What I've come to discover about my divine purpose is that it's more about my *'being'* and *'becoming'* more like Christ over my *'doing'* more for Christ. It's more about my *'abiding'* rather than my *'arriving'* (John 15:7-9). Purpose is more complex than all of that, yet it's also *as simple* as that.

Purpose is more about our 'being' over our 'doing'

In a nutshell, *purpose is what we step into by our daily surrender and obedience to God.* And just because God's purpose for your life is not always obvious or revealed to you, *it doesn't mean it isn't being fulfilled in and through you!*

Disney World was a dream vacation destination and God made a way for our family to go in 2022 and 2023! Growing up in poverty, I didn't believe a trip to Disney would be possible. But God made this dream come true! Twice! Pictured above, EPCOT (Disney's 100th year celebration) and on page 8, Disney Springs, FL.

God's PURPOSE for your life is not a destination. It's not a place you arrive to and then check the box.

I pray you'll recognize that **God is fulfilling His purposes and plans for your life right now** (Jeremiah 29:11). You just need to believe it BY FAITH—even if you can't understand it, see it, or even feel it at this moment.

When you recognize the step you're in TODAY is PURPOSE-FULL, you'll find yourself walking in that step with more joy, peace, hope, fulfillment, and contentment. I'm a living testimony.

RETHINK:

What do I need to rethink when it comes to *"becoming"* more like Christ versus *"doing"* more for Christ?

_____

_____

_____

_____

_____

REFLECT:

- How have I been limiting God's purposes to a future destination?
- How could God be fulfilling His divine purposes in my life right *now*?
- What is God wanting me to surrender so I can walk in step with His leading, timing and methods?

_____

_____

_____

_____

RESOLVE:

I will practice *abiding* in Christ *over arriving* to a desired destination by

_____

_____

REMEMBER

Purpose is what you step into by your daily obedience and surrender to God.

PRAY:

Father, I recognize your purpose for my life is not a destination I arrive to. Forgive me for being focused on my arriving instead of my abiding in you. Help me to walk in the purpose-full step you have me in today and help me trust YOU will fulfill your purpose for my life, especially when I doubt or feel afraid. I know you're ordering my steps and I'm confident that the good work you started in me will be carried on to completion until the day of Christ Jesus. I ask all these things in Jesus' name, amen.

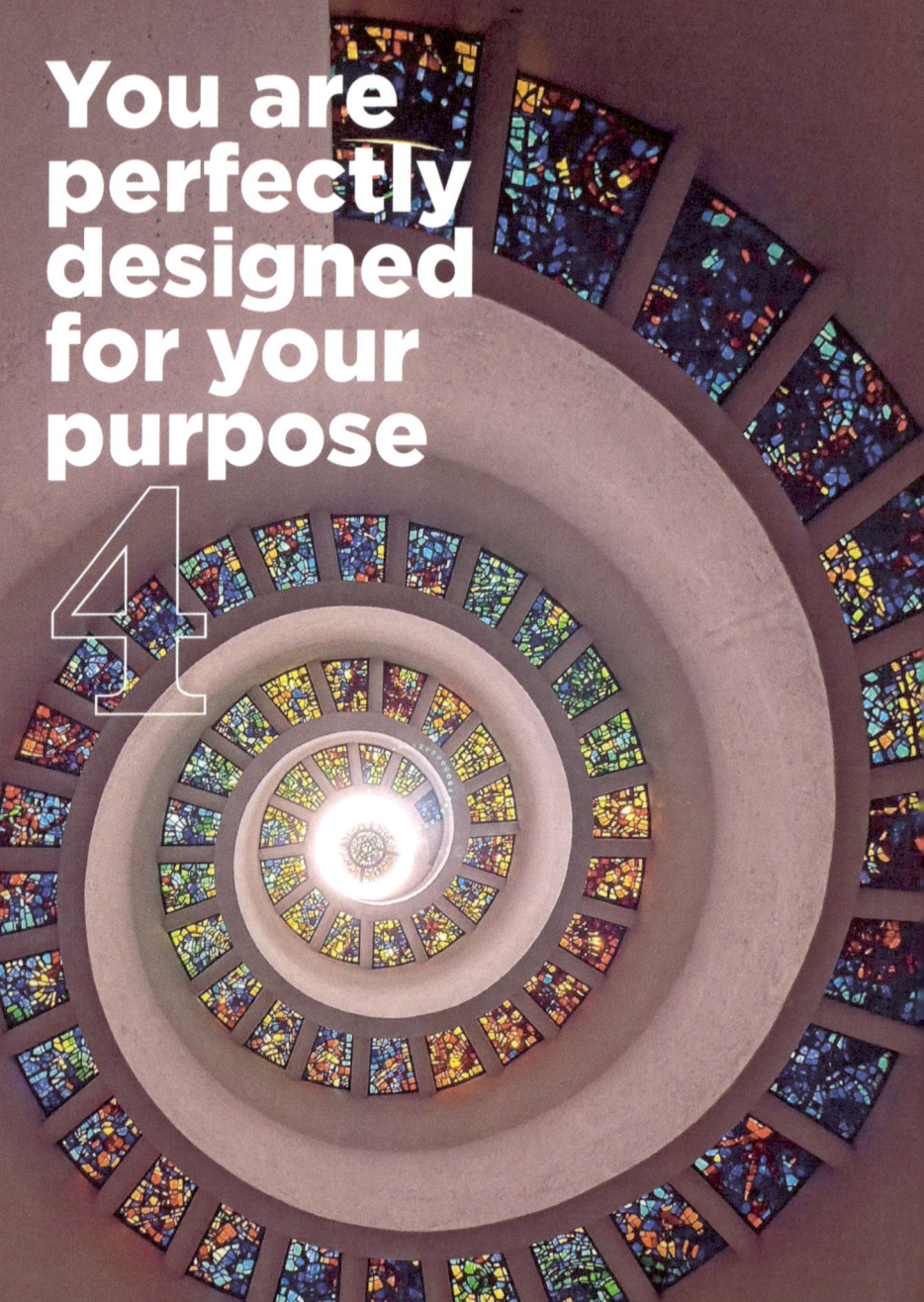

You are perfectly designed for your purpose

4

"The Glory Window", The Chapel of Thanksgiving, Dallas, TX, 2022.

For we are God's masterpiece. He has created us anew in Christ Jesus, so we can do the good things he planned for us long ago.

EPHESIANS 2:10 NLT

DID YOU KNOW YOU were divinely designed in the image of God (Genesis 1:27)? Yes! You have been uniquely equipped with unique gifts, talents, strengths, and abilities to demonstrate God's love and goodness in the world through good works and service. So this makes you FULL of divine GREATNESS!

Unfortunately, so many of God's children remain in the dark about how He has uniquely gifted them to serve and perform good works for His glory. Because they are unaware or lack the clarity on who God created them to be, many end up living below their God-given potential. When this happens, they're unable to confidently go out and impact the world in the remarkable ways God intended.

The enemy of your soul (Satan) doesn't want you to discover your divine design. He doesn't want you to discover your God-given gifts because he fears that in using them, you will devastate his kingdom.

If Satan can keep you in the dark concerning your divine greatness, or if he can trap you in analysis paralysis, constantly questioning and doubting your God-given gifts and power, he can delay your divine impact.

But that stops today! Today is the day you realize how God has intentionally, intricately, impeccably, and lovingly SHAPED you to live out His purpose for your life—before you were even conceived in your mother's womb! Talk about intentional divine design!!

In Jeremiah 1:5 (MSG) we see the Lord telling Jeremiah *"before I shaped you in the womb, I knew all about you."* I love how Pastor Rick Warren uses the acronym S.H.A.P.E.[1] to teach us how God has designed each of us with a unique S.H.A.P.E. *(spiritual gifts, heart or passions, abilities, personality and experiences)* to fulfill His purposes.

Just like no one else shares your fingerprint or footprint, no one else shares your unique S.H.A.P.E. You and I are a one of a kind, genuine masterpiece created in Christ Jesus! And we have been empowered with spiritual gifts to do good works (Ephesians 2:10) that build up the body of Christ toward maturity and equip the saints for works of ministry (Ephesians 4:12-13).

You are God's masterpiece.

I encourage you to discover the spiritual gifts you may have received when you accepted Christ as your personal Lord and Savior by studying Romans 12:6-8, 1 Corinthians 12:4-11 and 1 Corinthians 12:28. I also encourage you to discover your natural strengths, personality type, and passions to better understand your divine design. Remember, *you have been perfectly and purposely shaped (or divinely designed) with everything you need to live out your God-given purpose.* Be sure to check out Pastor Rick's free *S.H.A.P.E.* assessment at *www.freeshapetest.com* to discover *your* unique shape, as it may reveal aspects of your destiny!

Spiritual Gifts
Heart
Abilities
Personality
Experiences

OKC Myriad Botanical Gardens Illuminations: Starry, Starry Night, 2018.

RETHINK:
What do I need to rethink, know or understand about my divine design?

_____

_____

_____

_____

REFLECT:
How has God shaped me for His glory and purposes? What are some ways I can use my divine design to build up others in the body of Christ? What are some possible ways I can use my God-given S.H.A.P.E. to serve others for God's glory?

_____

_____

_____

_____

_____

_____

RESOLVE:
I won't compare my S.H.A.P.E. to others. I'll celebrate my unique S.H.A.P.E by

_____

_____

_____

_____

REMEMBER
You've been SHAPED with everything you need to live out your God-given purpose.

PRAY:
Father, thank you for being intentional in how you SHAPED me for your purposes. In all I do, I want my divine design to bring glory to you. Forgive me if I have ever coveted the S.H.A.P.E. of others, or compared my S.H.A.P.E. to that of others. Please teach me how to appreciate and celebrate the unique S.H.A.P.E. you have given me so I can boldly go and do all you have shaped me to do. I praise you because I am fearfully and wonderfully made. I ask all these things in Jesus' name, amen.

5 Prioritize God's vision over your plans

HAVE YOU EVER created a vision board *(or a visual representation)* of your goals and dreams? People use vision boards as a tool to motivate and inspire them to focus their attention and efforts on where they want to go and what they want to achieve. Vision boards help us imagine what our future could look like IF we work hard and stay focused on our goals.

One of the things I learned late in life is that a life lived without vision leads to a life without direction, passion, meaning, purpose, and significance. When I was younger, I used to ask myself:

"Where do you want to go in life?"

"What do you want to accomplish?"

Many are the plans in a person's heart,
but it is the Lord's purpose that prevails.

PROVERBS 19:21 NIV

But now that I've grown more kingdom-minded in my thinking, I ask God, *"What do you want me to accomplish for your kingdom?"* and *"What vision do you have in mind for me?"* As I look back over my life, I can see how the thoughts of my youth were very *"me-centered"* whereas my thoughts now are more *"God-centered."*

Now, you can certainly live out your own life vision and possibly be happy, but I don't believe you'll be completely fulfilled. Wouldn't life be so much more fulfilling, meaningful *(and eternally rewarding)* if you lived beyond yourself and followed God's vision over your plans?

But to know if our life vision aligns with God's vision, we must ask Him to divinely disclose what He has in mind for us.

When we study God's Word, we see examples of God disclosing His vision to Moses, Joseph and Abraham. God had a vision for Moses to be His chosen deliverer, the one to lead the Israelites out of Egyptian slavery and into the promised land (Exodus 3). God's vision for Abraham was to be the father of many nations (Genesis17:5). And God's vision for Joseph was to be an advisor and leader who would save countless lives during seven years of famine (Genesis 50).

Just as God had a specific vision and purpose in mind for these men, *He has a specific vision and purpose in mind for you* (Jeremiah 1:5).

A life lived without vision leads to a life without direction, passion, meaning, purpose and significance.

Knowing God's vision for your life serves as your compass because it sets the course and direction for all you do. But when you don't know God's vision for your life, you may find yourself chasing the wrong things and ending up at destinations He never intended for you. To avoid unnecessary detours and delays to your destiny, start asking God to disclose His vision for your life so you can prioritize His vision over your plans.

We must follow the example of Jesus by seeking to do the will of our Father, not our own (John 5:30). This must be our DESIRE. This must be our PRIORITY. This must be our FOCUS. And let me be clear. Doing the will of our Father will require us to deny ourselves *(our desires and ambitions)* and even die to some of our plans and dreams. But earthy rewards will never compare to the heavenly reward we'll receive for doing the will of our Father. Surrendering to God's plans doesn't guarantee we'll never experience pain or disappointment. Just look at the life of Job or Joseph in the Bible. But God does guarantee He'll never leave us or forsake us (Hebrews 13:5), and He promises to work out all the painful and disappointing experiences in our life for our good and for His glory (Romans 8:28; John 11:4).

Although God's vision for you is for an appointed time, and though it seems to tarry according to your perspective and time table, **choose to be of good courage** while you wait for God to bring it to pass (Habakkuk 2:3). **Choose to wait patiently** because God is always at work in your life as you wait (Psalms 37:3). And **choose to wait expectantly**, knowing God is able to do exceedingly and abundantly MORE than you could ever ask or think, according to the power that works in you (Ephesians 3:20).

GOD'S PLANS: *Growing up in poverty in McKees Rocks, PA, I never planned to see mountains like the Rocky Mountains in Colorado. But in 2022, God's plan took me there (see page 16). My plan never included leaving the city of Pittsburgh, but God's plan took me from living in PA, to Ohio, to Maryland, and now Oklahoma! (Red Rock Canyon State Park pictured at left (2021). What a wonderful adventure it has been!*

RETHINK:

What do I need to rethink when it comes to prioritizing God's vision over my plans?

_____

_____

_____

_____

REFLECT:

In what ways have I been seeking to fulfill my own vision above God's vision for me? What is God asking me to surrender so I can live out His vision for me?

_____

_____

_____

_____

_____

RESOLVE:

I will seek to know God's vision for my life and align my will and actions to His vision and plans for me.

PRAY:

Father, thank you for creating me on purpose, for a specific purpose. Help me to gain clarity on who you've created me to be so I can do all the things you've purposed me to do long ago. Father, I want to do your will above my own. Help me to surrender my plans to you so your purposes can prevail. I thank you for having plans to prosper me and not to harm me, plans to give me a future and a hope. Please help me to live out your vision and in turn bring glory to your name. I ask all this in Jesus' name, amen.

REMEMBER

God has a vision in mind for your life. But it's up to you to discover it.

Your mundane serves a purpose

HAVE YOU EVER FOUND yourself thinking, *"This is NOT the life I imagined for my self — a wayward spouse, a prodigal child, a difficult boss, a love that's been lost, or an unfulfilling job."* I have found myself time and time again thinking, *"Where I am is not where I want to be. This is not the dream I had in mind for me."*

Can you relate? If so, YOU ARE NOT ALONE. Just the other day, I was at work, sitting in my office cubicle, staring at the brick wall in front of me thinking, *"God, this is not the life I want to be living. This is not how I want to spend my life, boxed in a cubicle, typing on a laptop 8 hours a day. God I'm tired of this. This seems so pointless and mundane! This is not where I want to be because I know you have so much MORE for me."*

So here's what I want you to do, God helping you: Take your everyday, ordinary life—your sleeping, eating, going-to-work, and walking-around life—and place it before God as an offering.

ROMANS 12:1 MSG

And just as I had that thought, the Lord said to me, *"Radhika, you get to have the opportunity to be salt and light in your workplace. You get to be my ambassador of hope and goodness to all who cross your path. Don't you see I have planted you where you are on purpose for my purposes? Don't you see I am in all the things you perceive as mundane? Don't you see where I have placed you is by divine assignment? I have chosen you to represent me in your work. I have chosen you to do good works that bring glory to me. Don't you see? You get to present me to those around you so reframe how you see your ordinary "mundane" life. **Choose to see your life as one of divine purpose, divine placement and divine positioning.**"*

In that moment of reckoning, I decided to embrace my divine assignment and remember I'm a living letter of Christ for others to read, so they can encounter Jesus through me (2 Corinthians 3:1-3).

Friend, I know your everyday, ordinary life—your *"sleeping, eating, going-to-work, and walking-around life"* can feel mundane at times. I know it can feel like you aren't living a life full of meaning, purpose or significance. But the Word of God tells us in Romans 12:1-2 to take what **we perceive** as a mundane life and place it before God as an offering. We are called to **embrace** what God does for us. This means we must **willingly** and **enthusiastically accept** what God is doing in our lives—especially when we don't understand His plans, and especially when our reality fails to meet our expectations.

So the next time you think *"God, where is your purpose in my mundane life?"* choose to take your ordinary life and place it all before God as an offering.

Pictured above, this beautiful lantern caught my eye at The Battery in Charleston, SC. Pictured left, wild flowers at Mitch Park, Edmond, OK. I love visiting different parks and urban green spaces to recharge in nature because there is something so marvelous, miraculous and mesmerizing about all of God's creation.

A work trip in 2023 allowed me to tour The Battery in Charleston, SC. Pictured on page 21 & 22.

Choose to fix your attention on God, no matter *where* He's planted you and no matter *what* He has assigned you to do. When you embrace where God has you, you position yourself to receive MORE of His blessings. Here's one more nugget to chew on: *all* of your work, whether it is unpaid domestic labor *(such as household chores)*, raising children, or working in secular spaces, is spiritual work because you have the Spirit of God *in* you. Please don't miss God in what you perceive as mundane because ***"The quickest way for God to get you to where He wants you, is for Him to be able to use you where He has you." (Dr. Tony Evans, Twitter, Feb. 9, 2022)***

> **"**
>
> The quickest way for God to get you to where He wants you, is for Him to be able to use you where He has you."
>
> *Dr. Tony Evans*

RETHINK:
What do I need to reframe when it comes to the *seemingly* mundane in my life?

_____

_____

_____

_____

REFLECT:
What would it look like for me to place my *"ordinary sleeping, eating, going-to-work, and walking-around life"* before God as an offering?

_____

_____

_____

_____

RESOLVE:
I will focus my attention on God and embrace where He has placed me knowing I am in a place of divine purpose and positioning.

PRAY:
Father, thank you for ordering my steps. Help me to embrace where you have placed me, especially when it seems so mundane and insignificant. I know I don't always recognize the divine purpose in what I'm doing or where I'm planted so please help me to readily recognize your will and respond to it quickly and joyfully. I thank you for being my Good Shepherd, the One who restores my soul and leads me in the paths of righteousness for your name sake. I ask all this in Jesus' name, amen.

REMEMBER
Embracing where God has placed you keeps you in His place of purpose. And there's nothing mundane about that at all.

Your life disruptions serve a divine purpose

And we know that in all things God works for the good of those who love him, who have been called according to his purpose.

ROMANS 8:28 NIV

RECENTLY I had my mammogram exam. Unfortunately, I failed to make these screenings a priority over the past few years *(as routine screenings should start at 40 years of age)* but that has recently changed for me. As I have been taking major action to improve my overall health and well-being *(which includes prioritizing my annual check-ups)*, I can't stop thinking about a very good friend of mine who was diagnosed with breast cancer. I can only imagine how much this diagnosis disrupted her world.

"Alice in Wonderland" on scratchboard by John Cruz

And although my friend is full of faith, fire, and fight, it doesn't change the fact that she is experiencing a major life-quake.

As I've been thinking about the faith-filled, resilient spirit of my long-time sister-friend, I undoubtedly know it is BECAUSE of her faith in God that she is at peace. She has placed her life in the hands of the one and only PRINCE OF PEACE: JESUS. It is HE and only He, who has given her this peace that surpasses all understanding. THIS peace is her blessed assurance. It guards her heart and mind, and it's because of this supernatural peace that she presses on with faith and fight—confident that her faith in God will make her well (Mark 5:34).

As I reflected on how my friend coped with this plot twist in her life, it reminded me of how Jesus told us we would have troubles *(life-quakes, trials, and disruptors)* in life, but we are encouraged to take heart because He has overcome the world (John 16:33).

It also reminded me of a book I read called *"Life is in the Transitions"* by Bruce Feiler[2]. Bruce defines LIFE-DISRUPTORS as *"the events and experiences that interrupt the everyday flow of our life."* He chose the word "disruptor' *"as opposed to stressors, crises, problems, or any other label because the term is more value-neutral."*

Bruce goes on to say life-disruptors, such as adopting a child or starting a new job, are not traditionally defined as negative, but they are still disruptive because they interrupt the flow of one's life.

Feiler devised a list *(or as he calls it a deck)* of life-disruptors which includes 5 major life areas: **Love, Identity, Beliefs, Work and Body.** For example, disruptors in the **love** arena of our lives includes the death of a

What happens when your fairytale goes awry?

spouse, the divorce of parents, infertility, getting married, and divorce. Disruptors in the **work** arena include changing jobs, losing and/or quitting a job, entering retirement, or receiving significant public recognition (i.e., TED talk, award).

I truly believe life-disruptors can make us **better** or **bitter**. According to Bruce, our resilience depends on our ability to **"re-imagine, rethink, reconstruct, and rewrite our personal stories as things change, disrupt, or go 'wrong' in our lives."** I would add that our resilience also depends on the depths of our faith and hope — or God-confidence. To put it another way, our ability to bounce back *and better* from adversity is connected to our belief that God is always at work in our lives. It's anchored in knowing God will cause ALL things to work together for the good of those who love Him. Even when we don't understand. Even when we are in pain and are full of fear and anxiety. Even when things seem hopeless. And even when we walk through the valley of the shadow of death.

One powerful question Feiler poses in his book is *"What happens when your fairy tales go awry? What happens when there is a plot twist in your life?"* My question to you is: Do you stay stuck in anger, asking God why? *"Why me God? Why now?"* Or do you ask God, *"What now? How do you want me to respond to this life disruptor?"* Do you ask yourself, *"Will I allow this disruptor to define me and doom me?"* Or, *"Will I allow this to refocus me and reconstruct me? Will I allow it to grow my faith, my God-confidence, my perspective and my God-dependence?"* My dear friend....

What plot twists or life-quakes are you experiencing right now? What life-disruptors are you navigating? Maybe you're dealing with the loss of a spouse, friend, or loved one. Or perhaps you're facing the loss of a job or a business. Maybe it's the illness of your child or the grief of having a prodigal child. Maybe it's a recent health diagnosis or a recent decline in your physical mobility or ability. Maybe it's the inability to conceive a child, a marital separation, or a geographic relocation.

The reality is that *life will NOT always ascend*. Life is FULL of plot twists and turns. It's full of peaks and valleys, successes and setbacks, good surprises and stressors. It's full of triumphs and failures, joy and sorrow, pain and pleasure.

The reality is, life-disruptors have the ability to disorient us or destabilize us — if we give them the power to do so. According to Feiler, the key to being resilient and bouncing back from life's disruptors stronger and wiser is choosing to *"accept those life-disruptors, name them, mark them, share them and eventually convert them into a new and vital fuel for remaking our life stories."*

Bruce goes on to say that *"Life is the story you tell yourself. But how you tell that story, as a hero, victim, lover, warrior, caretaker, believer, matters a great deal. How you adapt that story, how you*

revise, rethink and rewrite your personal narrative as things change, lurch or go wrong in your life—matters even more."

Would you agree? What story are you telling yourself about your life-disruptors? *If the story you've been telling yourself contradicts God's story, His ability to use life-disruptors for your good, you're in the wrong story*.

WE MAY NEVER KNOW WHY SOMETHING BAD HAPPENS IN OUR LIFE BUT WE CAN REST ASSURED KNOWING GOD IS FOR US, NOT AGAINST US.

Decide to get into God's story. No matter the disruptive event or experience you're facing, you have a choice. You can perceive your disruptive event as an opportunity to grow your faith and invite God to show himself strong in your life, OR you can perceive it as something you'll never heal from or overcome—something God is not able to use for your good or His glory.

The good news is YOU have the ability to get a 'God-perspective' by focusing on what God is able to do for you and through you in the face of your life-disruptors. I truly believe *your resilience is rooted in your belief that God is still good, even when bad things happen.*

And your resilience is rooted in believing that nothing can separate you from the love of God, and nothing happens to you in life without His permission. Your resilience is also rooted in knowing God's ways are so much higher than your ways, and it also involves choosing to accept you may never know why something bad has happened in your life. It's about resting in the truth that *no matter what you face, God is with you and for you,* and He will give you the strength to face any life-disruptor that comes your way. As I keep on living, I've discovered my resilience is rooted in the truth that my life, health, family, and future are ultimately in God's hands. And there are no better hands I want to be in. How about you?

RETHINK:
What do I need to reframe when it comes to my life-disruptors?

_____

_____

REFLECT:
How can I frame my life story in a way that depicts God's presence, power, purpose, protection and provision in the midst of my life-disruptors?

_____

_____

RESOLVE:
I will place all my faith, hope and trust in God when I experience life disruptions knowing He will work them all out for my good.

PRAY:
Lord I thank you for being the author and finisher of my faith. Please help me to gain your perspective on every challenge and life-disruptor I face. Help me to remain confident in what you're able to do when I face trials and troubles. Lord help me to remember that my momentary troubles are achieving for me an eternal glory that far outweighs all my life-disruptors. Thank you for always working things together for my good, even when I may not see it or feel it. I ask all this in Jesus' name, amen.

REMEMBER
Your resilience is rooted in believing God is *still* good even when bad things happen.
(Romans 8:28).

Your Perspective

OBTAIN THE MIND OF CHRIST SO YOU MAY KNOW AND UNDERSTAND GOD'S PLAN, PURPOSE, AND PERSPECTIVE.

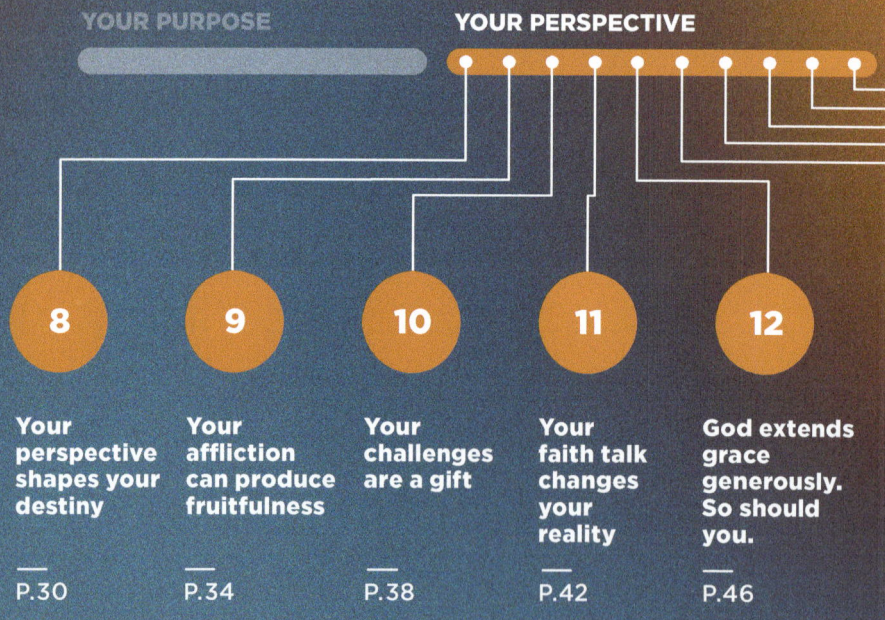

"Your perspective shapes your life."

Radhika Cruz

8

Your perspective shapes your destiny

So then, it was not you who sent me here, but God.

GENESIS 45:8 NIV

I'M ALWAYS AMAZED TO HEAR STORIES OF PEOPLE WHO WHILE imprisoned, find the motivation and grit to obtain a college degree, join a professional soccer team or win a gold medal as a member of an international choir. Recently I read an article[3] about a man currently serving 25 years-to-life in prison. He described prison as a place where *"the lack of privacy is emotionally exhausting, the empty nature of prison friendships is socially unfulfilling. The boredom is mind-numbing. The loneliness can be crushing, and the inflexible power structure embeds anger into one's personality."*

Pictured left, Rocky Mountain National Park. Above, bird viewer at Martin Park Nature Center, OKC. Page 32, Crystal Bridge Conservatory, OKC. Tip: Ask God to give you His perspective on your experiences.

But in this article, this young man said something so profound about being sentenced to life in prison. He said *"How I view my situation will determine how I live while I'm here. I am NOT the victim."* Wow. To be imprisoned and somehow not be full of despair, regret, and anguish is unimaginable to me. What a hope-full perspective on what is often perceived to be a hopeless situation. Talk about finding hope in a hopeless place.

When I think about someone in the Bible who also experienced the pain and trauma of incarceration, loneliness and loss of family, I think of Joseph (Genesis 37-45). Because of sibling rivalry and jealousy, Joseph was plotted against by his own brothers and left for dead at their hands, sold into slavery, and later imprisoned for a crime he didn't commit. He was abused, falsely accused, and wrongfully imprisoned because the justice system failed him.

Joseph *could've* viewed himself as a victim. He *could've* taken on the identity of a slave or criminal. He *could've* viewed his life as one that wasn't prospering or full of hope. He *could've* allowed his experiences to make him bitter, unforgiving, unkind, untrusting, and uncaring.

His life experiences *could've* caused him to believe he was helpless, unloved and unwanted—and without power, potential, or purpose. Joseph *could've* lost all faith, hope, and trust in God AND people. He *could've* chose to be, and stay offended—especially toward those who harmed him. He *could've* chose to become an oppressor and repay evil for evil. **But he didn't.**

Check out Genesis 45:4-8 where we learn of Joseph's perspective as he reveals his true identity to his brothers who had *no idea* he was still alive. They are about to see how Joseph not only survived their death trap

but thrived *despite* it! In this passage, Joseph says to his brothers:

"I am your brother Joseph, the one you sold into Egypt! And now, do not be distressed and do not be angry with yourselves for selling me here, because it was to save lives that God sent me ahead of you. For two years now there has been famine in the land, and for the next five years, there will be no plowing and reaping. But God sent me ahead of you to preserve for you a remnant on earth and to save your lives by a great deliverance. So then, it was not you who sent me here, but God. He made me a father to Pharaoh, lord of his entire household and ruler of all Egypt."

The golden nugget we gain from this passage is: Joseph didn't see himself as being *sold* into slavery. He saw himself as being *sent* by God to *save* lives. Although Joseph acknowledged the painful reality of how his brothers meant to harm him by leaving him for dead, he chose to forgive AND bless them instead (Genesis 45:8-24). Joseph viewed his hardships through the lens of God's omniscience and omnipotence.

How many of us can see the divine plan and purpose behind our painful experiences? Joseph mastered the art of seeing things from God's vantage point. Learning how to obtain a godly perspective on our suffering is a spiritual practice we can all grow in.

And if God caused Joseph to prosper in the land of his sorrow (Genesis 41:50-5), He can do the same for you and me! Ask God to give you His perspective on your painful experiences because when you have His perspective, you'll no longer look at things the same. *Remember, if God allowed something painful to enter your life story, you can trust He intends to use it for your good, AND His glory* (Romans 8:28). That's HIS promise to me and you!

RETHINK:
What painful life experiences do I need to reframe as something God will use (or is using) for my good and His divine purpose?

_____

_____

_____

REFLECT:
How have I allowed myself to be stuck in a negative self-story as a victim? In what ways can I see God using my pain for His purposes, my good, and the good of others?

_____

_____

_____

RESOLVE:
I will no longer see myself as a victim because God always turns my pain into something purpose-full.

PRAY: *Father help me to see that every pressure, hardship, and rejection that happened to me will be used for my good, your purpose, and your glory. Thank you for using my pain to accomplish your divine purpose. When trials come my way, help me to see it as divine positioning. Help me to remember that you turn around evil human intentions and work them for my good. Thank you for turning my pain into purpose and prospering me in the midst of my sorrow, suffering and adversity. I ask all this in Jesus name, amen.*

REMEMBER
Your perspective makes all the difference.

9

Your affliction can produce fruitfulness

For God has made me fruitful in the land of my affliction.

GENESIS 41:52 ESV

HAVE YOU EVER EXPERIENCED A CRISIS—A TIME OF INTENSE difficulty in your life? Maybe your crisis involved receiving a negative medical report or the loss of a relationship, home, job, or means of transportation. In the early years of my marriage, I experienced the loss of income which led to the loss of my utilities and transportation due car repossession. This was an especially difficult time in my marriage. And although I don't wish it on anyone, these crises presented me with the opportunity to grow in my faith and dependence on God to provide for all of my needs.

When written in Mandarin, the word crisis is comprised of two characters. One character represents *danger*, and the other represents *opportunity*. I believe a crisis always presents us with an opportunity to grow, innovate, change, and elevate. During a crisis, we can choose to pivot or panic, grow or grieve, hope or despair. But do we always choose to maximize the growth opportunities in our crisis situations?

CRISIS ALWAYS PRESENTS AN OPPORTUNITY FOR US TO GROW, INNOVATE, CREATE, CHANGE AND ELEVATE.

When facing crises, I remind myself that it's not just an opportunity for me to SURVIVE through it, it's an opportunity for me to THRIVE through it. If I want to GROW through crises, I MUST LEARN how to *"Expect the best, prepare for the worst and maximize what comes."* (Zig Ziglar).

Pictured on page 34, Eisenhower State Park on Lake Texoma, TX (2017) and pictured above, Myriad Botanical Gardens, OKC (2016). If you haven't already noticed, I am a nature enthusiast!

One biblical character who found himself in crisis quite often was Joseph. In Genesis 41:50-52, we read how he lost his identity, family, culture, and freedom because his brothers (who were jealous of him) threw him into a pit to die. Here's a man who lost everything. BUT GOD was with him. Even though he was wrongfully imprisoned and enslaved, God caused everything he did to prosper (Genesis 39:2). No person, place or experience could stop God from prospering Joseph — no trauma, imprisonment, familial rejection, or enslavement. NOTHING! God's caused Joseph to prosper (be fruitful) in the land of his sorrow (Genesis 41:50-52). And as a way to remind himself of God's favor on his life, Joseph named his second son Ephraim, which means "**Double Prosperity**."

I believe the most important opportunity we can maximize during a crisis is the opportunity to strengthen our relationship with God. When we intentionally connect with God during a crisis through prayer,

THE MOST IMPORTANT OPPORTUNITY WE CAN MAXIMIZE DURING A CRISIS IS THE OPPORTUNITY TO STRENGTHEN OUR RELATIONSHIP WITH GOD.

worship, and the reading of His word, our faith increases, our hope rises, our joy is made complete, and our peace is made perfect. In short, we strengthen our faith (1 Peter 1:7), grow in our character (James 2:3), and see things from a higher or spiritual perspective (Isaiah 55:8-9).

How wonderful to know that in our times of sorrow, lack, loss, difficulty, sickness, and sadness, God is MORE than able to give us a double portion of prosperity; therefore, we can still flourish and be very fruitful!

RETHINK:
What do I need to rethink concerning my crisis, pain, loss or adversities?

_____

_____

_____

REFLECT:
What fruit (or good things) have come from my crises and painful life experiences? How have I become better, wiser, stronger and more resilient?

_____

_____

_____

RESOLVE:
God will give me a double portion of peace and prosperity in times of pain, adversity, crisis and sorrow.

PRAY:
Father, I thank you for making all grace abound to me, so that in all things, at all times, you give me everything I need and more to abound in every good work you've called me to perform. Please help me to focus my eyes on your character, power and provision when facing trials and tribulations. Thank you for who you are and for blessing me at all times. I choose to bless you at all times and your praise will continually be in my mouth, no matter the season or situation I may face. I ask all these things in Jesus' name, amen.

REMEMBER
Prosperity does not depend on your situations or seasons. It depends on God's character, favor and kindness.

10

Your challenges are a gift

> *Consider it a sheer gift, friends, when tests and challenges come at you from all sides. You know that under pressure, your faith-life is forced out into the open and shows its true colors.*
>
> JAMES 1:2-4 MSG

HAVE YOU EVER TRIED TO peel a hard boiled egg with the goal of having the shell come off in one large piece? Before I adopted a whole food plant-based lifestyle, I used to eat hard boiled eggs for lunch. On one particular occasion, I tried to peel my egg shell off in one piece but to no avail. I had to patiently break off the shell little by little, bit by bit. I was frustrated with this tedious process because I was extremely hungry and wanted to eat immediately, but in my moment of frustration, I heard God say,

"Just as you need to be patient in breaking off the egg shell bit by bit to avoid destroying the egg, likewise, you must be patient with the breaking process I have you in. The process you're in will seem slow and a bit tedious to you but if it's rushed, it will not yield the beautiful outcome I intend. So endure the challenging process I have you in right now knowing it will produce more richer fruit in the end."

At that time, I was experiencing a season of immense frustration and disappointment. My life was not turning out the way I had expected, and I was extremely discouraged and discontent—so much so I thought it would be better if I no longer existed.

But God used a hard boiled egg to remind me of how He does a great inner work in us, bit by bit, little by little. So often we want to avoid or expedite our growth process, but He wants us to endure tests and challenges with faith, hope and patience — and consider them nothing but a joy and a gift! I don't know about you but I don't typically consider it a joy or gift when I face challenges on all sides.

The truth is, in order for us to be mature in our faith, we must let God take us through a breaking process. Just as a seed must go through the process of being broken

Pictured left and on page 40, Balboa Park Lily Pond, San Diego, California (2018). Orchids and Calla Lily's are my favorite flowers. In Christian theology, the spots on orchids symbolize the blood of Christ.

39

to produce fruit, we too must go through a process of being broken by enduring challenges, set-backs, and disappointments, dying to old habits, and renewing our minds and emotions. But the quality and magnitude of our fruitfulness is determined by how we **respond** to tests and challenges — the divine tools God uses to transform us into who He desires us to be. When your faith is tested, and you face challenges on all sides, do you count it all joy and endure patiently, or do you despise it grudgingly? Do you see your challenges as gifts—as gateways to your growth? Do you lean into them with a sense of expectancy for the rich fruit that'll be produced as a result of enduring your tests? Or do you see your challenges as obstacles you'll never overcome?

What faith testing and pruning process does God have you in right now? What challenges and pressures is He using to grow your faith, shift your perspective, and develop your character? Is He using relational rejection and disappointment, job loss, sickness, financial hardship, or loneliness?

No matter the test or challenge God uses to grow your faith and character, you are to consider it a joy and gift because, *as you're tested and spiritually pruned, God restores your soul and makes you stronger, firmer, and more steadfast in your faith.* What a gift! Dear friend, the next time you find yourself faced with challenges on all sides, rest assured knowing the Divine Gardener is pruning you (breaking you) to produce *richer* and *more excellent fruit* for your good, AND His glory (John 15:2-8). So trust God's breaking process, tools, and timing because your fruitfulness is ALWAYS His goal!

RETHINK:
What do I need to reframe when it comes to the challenges and pressures I'm facing?

_____

_____

_____

_____

REFLECT:
What areas of my life does God want me to produce more fruit in? What tests, challenges and pressures is He using to help me grow in my faith, hope, love, joy, peace, patience, generosity, gentleness, kindness or self-control?

_____

_____

_____

_____

RESOLVE:
I will embrace God's breaking process because it will grow my faith, develop my character, and cause me to produce richer, more excellent fruit for God.

PRAY:
Father, I thank you for using challenges and pressure to develop my character and grow my faith. Help me to let you do your work in me so I will produce much fruit for your glory. I thank you that your grace is sufficient for me and that your power is made perfect in my weakness. Lord, help me to remain in you and in your process so I can bear much fruit for your glory and show the world I am your disciple. I ask these things in Jesus's name, amen.

REMEMBER

Let challenges and pressure do its work in you so you can become mature and well-developed.

11
Your faith talk changes your reality

> *"...Take courage, daughter, your personal trust
> and confident faith in Me has made you well."*
>
> MATTHEW 9:22 AMP

D ID YOU KNOW YOUR SELF-talk or internal dialogue affects your self-esteem, self-worth, self-confidence and self-image? It also influences your patterns of thinking and acting, your habits, *and* your character. In short, your self-talk *(also called your self-stories or internal script)* shapes every area of your life because **you become and do what you repeatedly think.** There are 3 common yet powerful types of self-talk that have the ability to influence your life in a positive or negative direction. *Which type of self-talk do you find yourself in the most?*

3 TYPES OF SELF-TALK:

1. Negative Self-Talk:
This type of inner dialogue is discouraging and damaging. It sounds like: "I'm not good enough," "I'm stupid," "I'm a failure," or "I can't" or "I'm not good at this."

2. Positive Self-Talk:
This type of inner dialogue is useful and helpful. It sounds like: "I will do better next time," "Failure is success in progress," or "I can do hard things."

3. Possibility Self-Talk:
This type of inner dialogue is full of optimism and hope. It sounds like: "What if I can do ____?" or "What can this become?" or "How can I get this done?"

What we say to ourselves has the power to free us and heal us, OR enslave us and hinder us. But we thrive most when our self-talk is full of faith talk, and not just positive self-talk.

> **FAITH TALK IS WHEN OUR INTERNAL DIALOGUE COMMUNICATES ASSURANCE OF THINGS HOPED FOR IN THE ABSENCE OF EVIDENCE.**

Faith talk is having **unwavering** confidence in the power, wisdom, and goodness of God to do exceedingly and abundantly above all we could ever ask for, think, or imagine. Faith talk is believing "I will" or "I can" because of the great 'I AM.'

A great example of faith talk can be seen in the life of a woman who had been bleeding for 12 years (Matthew 9). As a woman, I know how uncomfortable, inconvenient and irritating it is to bleed for five days straight each month for decades— but to bleed *every single day* for 12 years straight? My God!

I can't imagine the frustration and agony this woman must have felt as she spent all her time, energy, and money searching for a cure to no avail. But here are a few things I learned from this woman's story:

- **Her internal dialogue reflected *continuous* faith talk:** she had been saying to herself *"If I only touch his outer robe, I will be healed." (Matthew 9:21)*

- **Her faith talk led her to act in faith:** she chose to press through a crowd to touch Jesus, *despite* cultural norms that prohibited her from entering public spaces, such as the temple, because she was considered *'ceremonially unclean'*.

- **Her faith talk AND faith walk led to her healing:** it was her confident faith in Jesus' power PLUS her faith in action of touching Jesus' garment, *despite the social rules of her time*, that led to her miraculous healing. She had a faith mindset that believed **"With God, there's always a way, and by faith, I will find it."**

I'm not sure if this woman's mindset was ALWAYS full of faith because she did spend all of her money trusting doctors to make her well, but in this moment of desperation, *her faith talk AND faith action turned her hope of being healed into her reality.* Because of her personal trust and confident faith in Jesus' ability to heal her, she was instantly healed.

When you place your trust in God's power to perform a miracle in your life and choose to step out in faith through some sort of action, then you will know what it means to live by faith. And you will see God come through in your seemingly impossible situations according to your faith.

Remember, with God, **ALL** things are possible if you believe. It's your job to **believe** what you ask for by faith, and it's God's job to **respond** to your faith in His time and way. So choose to talk walk by faith, and expect your miracle because it's surely on the way!

RETHINK:
What do I need to change when it comes to my self-talk *(my inner narrative and self-stories)*?

_____

_____

_____

_____

REFLECT:
What faith talk do I need to commit to speaking? What faith action do I need to take?

_____

_____

_____

_____

RESOLVE:
My self-talk will be FULL of faith, as will my actions, because with God, there's always a way and by faith, I will find it.

PRAY:
Father I am so thankful you are able to do exceedingly and abundantly above all I could ever ask or imagine. Please help me to remember that nothing is too hard for you and that all things are possible if I believe. Father help my unbelief and help me to not only declare your truth by faith, but to also live by faith because I know that without faith, it is impossible to please you. I ask all these things in Jesus's name, amen.

REMEMBER
It is your faith talk AND your faith walk that creates space for God to do the miraculous in your life.

Pictured left and on page 42, Grand Lake, Rocky Mountain National Park (2022). This was my first time visiting the Rockies with my big brother and bonus sister. This is the longest mountain range in all of North America. What a wildlife paradise!

God extends grace gener- ously.

12

SO SHOULD YOU.

Don't repay evil for evil. Don't retaliate with insults when people insult you. Instead, pay them back with a blessing. That is what God has called you to do, and he will grant you his blessing.

1 PETER 3:9 NLT

HAVE YOU EVER BEEN LIED ON, TALKED bad about, or mistreated by someone? I have and let me tell you my flesh immediately wants to clap back by returning verbal insults for emotional injury. What about you? How do YOU respond when someone mistreats you, despises you, wrongly accuses you, or uses you for their selfish gain? I don't know about you, but if I'm not careful to guard my heart, it can quickly fill up with anger, resentment, bitterness and unforgiveness. To put it another way, I can easily find myself complaining and gossiping about those who have wronged me instead of praying for them, extending grace to them, and forgiving them.

The Bible reminds us *"all have sinned and fall short of God's glory"* (Romans 3:23). That includes me and you. But let's be real. It's hard to refrain from defending ourselves when we feel wrongfully attacked or insulted. So how *should* you respond when people insult you or act hatefully toward you? 1 Peter 3:9 tells us *"Do not repay evil for evil. Don't retaliate with insults when people insult you. Instead, pay them back with a blessing. That is what God has called you to do, and he will grant you his blessing."*

Wait, what? Pay them back with a *blessing*? That's the complete opposite of what my flesh wants to do! But did you know that paying back someone who has done you wrong *with a blessing* is an act of biblical obedience and grace?

Grace by definition is undeserved kindness. It's paying others back by:

- Extending kindness to those who've hurt you

- Giving the benefit of the doubt and assuming positive intent rather than malicious intent

- Extending forgiveness without limit or condition

- Overlooking an offense and praying for those who spitefully use and persecute you

- Doing good to those who hate/despise you

- Refraining from lashing out with gossip and slander

Pictured above, Estes Park, Rocky Mountain National Park (2022). Pictured on page 46, Will Rogers Gardens, OKC (2017).

It's so easy to repay evil for evil and vilify those who have hurt or disappointed us in some way. It's much easier to turn away from or against those who have caused us emotional injury because they aren't *'perfect and sinless'* like us, right? *(insert sarcasm here)*. It's easy to sit in a judgment seat of self-righteousness and believe we are better than those who act in unkind and insulting ways. And it's so easy to stay offended, ruminating on all the hurt someone has caused us, remaining bitter, angry, and defensive, isn't it?

But when we have this type of heart posture toward others, we operate from a place of judgment, condemnation, and unforgiveness rather than a heart posture of grace, forgiveness and kindness, which God desires. All of us can do better with cultivating more grace toward those who have hurt us. When we can learn to overlook offenses and forgive quickly and endlessly, we will experience the same measure of grace and forgiveness extended **right back to us** because we indeed reap what we sow (Galatians 6:7-9).

When you've been mistreated by others, you need God's strength to resist the urge for revenge. And because people are imperfect and sinful, you are guaranteed to be hurt, humiliated and mistreated in life. But God's way is to be kind, tenderhearted, compassionate and forgiving towards others as He is to **you**. His want us to freely extend grace since we have freely received it from Him as a gift. God's way of how we are to respond is counterintuitive and counter-cultural, but this is the way He wants you, me, and **all** His children to live.

RETHINK:
What do I need to rethink when it comes to my posture toward those who have mistreated, insulted or harmed me?

_____

REFLECT:
What would it look like for me to generously extend grace to those who have hurt me? Who is God asking me to extend His grace to?

_____

_____

RESOLVE:
I refuse to retaliate against those who hurt me and despise me. I'll instead pay them back with a blessing of love and kindness.

PRAY:
Father, I thank you for your grace which is greater than all my sin. Please help me to not repay evil for evil but instead, repay evil with love, grace and kindness. Help me to pray for my enemies, those who use me, mistreat me, and lie about me. God help me resist the urge and tendency to defend myself because you are my defense. Thank you for causing my enemies to be at peace with me as I live in way that pleases you. I ask these things in Jesus' name, amen.

> **REMEMBER**
> Love your enemies and pray for those who mistreat you, use you and persecute you.
>
> MATTHEW 5:44

Placing your hope in God anchors your life

"For I know the plans I have for you," declares the Lord,
"plans to prosper you and not to harm you,
plans to give you hope and a future."

JEREMIAH 29:11 NIV

13

A S A TEEN GROWING UP IN AN INNER-CITY HOUSING PROJECT outside of Pittsburgh, PA, I would often look out of my bedroom window and think **"I'm going to die here."** At that time in my life, I didn't have any hope for my future. Life felt meaningless, purposeless and directionless. I believed I was destined to live a life of poverty and insignificance rather than one of prosperity, purpose and significance. But when I met the God of hope, I received hope, and then EVERYTHING changed.

According to the science of hope, the best predictor of our success and well-being in life *is not* our intelligence quotient (IQ) or our emotional intelligence quotient (EQ). It's actually our hope quotient (HQ). Hope scientists define hope as *"the belief that my future can be better than today and I have the power to make it so."* (Chan Hellman, *Hope Rising*[4]). Hope research tells us that hope consists of 3 key components: *setting meaningful goals, identifying viable pathways* (waypower or strategies) for achieving our goals, and s*ustaining motivation to achieve our goals* (or willpower), especially when experiencing setbacks, challenges, or adversity. To simplify, hope consists of having a meaningful goal, willpower, and waypower.

Biblical hope is the confident expectation or trust we have in God (and not ourselves) to fulfill His good plans, purpose and promises for us.

However, if we look at hope from a *biblical* perspective, it's not simply about setting goals, optimistic thinking, or anticipating good outcomes. Biblical hope is the confident expectation and trust we have **in God** to fulfill His good plans, purpose, and promises for us (Jeremiah 29:11; Psalms 138:8). It's believing in and depending on **God's power and promise** to give us a future full of hope while we trust Him to make good on His word (Isaiah 40:31).

Biblical hope believes God will cause all things to work together for our good (Romans 8:28) and that He is directing our steps, initiating good things for us — things we can't accomplish on our own. It is having unwavering belief in God's ability to do what He has promised, despite the odds being stacked against us, despite our current reality, despite the facts we face, and despite dreams that seem unlikely to be fulfilled.

When we place all of our hope and trust in God, and when we wait **patiently**, **enthusiastically** and **expectantly** for Him to fulfill His purpose and promises in our lives, He renews our strength and power (Isaiah 40:31). And it is with this renewed power that we can confidently step into the unknown, daring to trust God to set things right for us, especially when things seem hopeless or beyond our ability to change (Romans 4:2-25 MSG).

If the situation you're facing today seems hopeless, if you think your future won't be brighter or better, or if you think you don't have the power to improve your circumstances, remember to place your

In my housing project outside of Pittsburgh, PA (above), I saw poverty, despair, crack dealers and crack users. I never imagined seeing mountains in places like the Rockies (pg. 42, 48) or the Wichita Mountains, OK (pg. 50).

hope and confidence in God's power and initiative (and not your's alone) to make your future better.

It is God's responsibility to make your future prosperous *(according to his definition of prosperity and not your own)*. But it's on YOU to commit your plans to God, follow His lead, and trust Him to bring His promises for your life to pass, especially when you think there's nothing to hope for (Jeremiah 29:11; Romans 4:18). Remember, biblical hope is not found in what you can achieve on your own. It's not found in your goals, motivation or waypower alone. Enduring hope is God-confidence, not self-confidence, because God is your waymaker and waypower. Biblical hope is completely trusting in God's power and promise to prosper you, direct you, and give you a better future.

You can choose to set goals and devise plans all you want, but it's the Lord's plan and purpose that will prevail in your life.

If you want to live an abundant life— a life full of joy, hope, meaning, purpose, and significance— commit your plans to God and trust in His power above your own to bring you to a future full of joy, peace, HOPE, purpose, and fulfillment.

RETHINK:

What do I need to rethink when it comes to where my hope comes from?

_____

_____

_____

_____

REFLECT:

What does it look like for me to receive God's gift of hope? How would my life be different if I chose to keep believing God has good plans for me and my future, even when I think there's no reason to hope?

_____

_____

_____

_____

RESOLVE:

I freely receive God's gift of hope to me and I place all my confidence in His power to make my future better, despite what I think is impossible or unlikely for my life.

PRAY:

Father, thank you for being the source of my hope. Please help me trust your plans to give me a hope and a future. From this day forward, I place all my confidence in your ability and promise to make my future better. And when I find myself doubting your purpose and plans for my life, strengthen my belief. I ask this in Jesus's name, amen.

READ MORE: Romans 4:18

REMEMBER

"God, the source of hope, will fill you completely with joy and peace because you trust in him. Then you will overflow with confident hope through the power of the Holy Spirit."
Romans 15:13

14

Your unplanned paths are divine redirection

S O OFTEN PEOPLE SAY HINDSIGHT IS 20/20 BECAUSE WHEN YOU look back at things that have happened in your life, you tend to see the purpose more clearly. This reminds me of the late Steve Jobs who said *"You can't connect the dots looking forward; you can only connect them looking backwards. So you have to trust that the dots will somehow connect in your future. You have to trust in something—your gut, destiny, life, karma, whatever."* I think Steve was onto something but as children of God, we place our trust in the Lord. He is the one who directs our steps and connects our dots according to His plan and purposes.

Our knowledge and understanding of why certain events and situations happen in our lives is limited, partial and incomplete (1 Corinthians 13:9). Although we may never know or understand *why* God allowed certain things to happen, we can trust He is connecting all the dots for the vision and purpose He has in mind for us. As you look back on some of the painful, disappointing, unexpected and unwanted experiences of your past, maybe you can now connect the dots and see the divine purpose in them. But this won't always be the case.

As someone who likes to create plans for my future, I can't help but look back over my life and laugh at how SO many of my plans have been divinely disrupted. For example, I had plans to marry a tall, Black man, but God had plans for me to marry a Puerto Rican man of average height instead (no shade babe!). And let me tell you, he's God's best earthly gift to me. I thought I knew what I needed, but God gave me who I needed.

I thought I knew what I needed but God gave me who I needed.

In my late teens, I had a plan to become a missionary overseas, but God planned for me to go on a few mission trips overseas instead. I had plans to retire from a career in child welfare in the state of Ohio, but God divinely disrupted my plan. Now I live in Oklahoma, a state I never desired to reside in, doing work in career I never planned or imagined but absolutely love! I also didn't plan on having any children, but I have two children who are among God's best gifts to me! I had planned to only work in secular spaces, but God had a plan for me to work in vocational ministry for a season, which was NEVER in my vision or career plan. However, those experiences grew my faith and character tremendously!

I could go on and on with more examples from my life of how God disrupted my plans but you get my point. Life doesn't turn out the way we plan because it's actually God who directs our steps to fulfill his plan, for He truly delights in every detail of our lives (Psalms 37:23)!

As I continue to grow in my walk with God and cry out for His perspective on what I perceive are '*disruptions*' to my plans, I become more and more aware of how they are not really disruptions at all. They are, instead, **divine redirections**.

As I look back over my life, I can see *(but only in part)* how God used the death of my mother, three geographic relocations, and three career changes to direct me toward fulfilling His purpose and plans for my life.

As you continue your journey with God, remember that perceived delays, detours and disruptions to your plans are actually *divine redirections*. God is *always* at work, connecting all your dots to fulfill the vision He has in mind for you. You may not be able to connect all the dots in your perceived detours, delays, or disruptions looking back, but you can rest assured knowing God is always at work fulfilling His dream and plan for your life.

You must remember it is God who directs your life, not you. So often we ask God for more clarity regarding the purpose of our unplanned paths when **all we need is more trust in the Lord.** You may chart a course for your life with your plans but remember it's God who directs your steps. Choose to commit your plans to God (Proverbs 16:3) and recognize that 'disruptions' to your plans are often *"divine redirection"* to the plans and purpose God has for your life.

I admire beautiful and unique architecture like the Arthur Ravenel Jr. Bridge in Charleston, SC (pg.54) and this beach pier at Folly Beach, SC (pg.57). On this work-related trip in 2023, I had so much fun exploring this beach and Sullivan's Island! What a wonderful job perk!

RETHINK:

What do I need to rethink when it comes to *perceived* disruptions to my plans?

_____

_____

REFLECT:

What plan, dream or expectation does God wants me to surrender to Him?

_____

_____

_____

RESOLVE:

I will embrace divine redirection in my life because God wants to use it to accomplish His plans and purpose for my life.

PRAY:

Father, thank you for delighting in every detail of my life and directing my steps toward your purposes. Please help me to view divine disruptions to my plans, as divine redirection to my next divine assignment. Lord, keep disrupting my plans so I can walk in your good and perfect plan for my life. I ask these things in Jesus' name, amen.

REMEMBER

Disruptions to your plans are often designed by God to direct your steps toward His purpose and plan for your life.

15

Your disappointments are divine appointments

> *Such hope (in God's promises) never disappoints us, because God's love has been abundantly poured out within our hearts through the Holy Spirit who was given us.*
>
> ROMANS 5:5 AMP

DISAPPOINTMENT. NOT A feeling or emotional state you want to experience or stay stuck in right? Disappointment can be defined as a feeling of sadness or loss concerning an outcome that didn't turn out the way you had expected, anticipated or hoped.

I'm sure you can look back over your life and recall some of your own disappointments. I remember experiencing disappointment in *friendships* because certain friends did not turn out to be as supportive or constant as I had expected. I've faced *career* disappointment in that my "dream job" did not turn out to be my dream job after all. And I've experienced disappointment in *prayer* because something I had prayed for, such as my mother being healed of cancer, didn't get answered the way I had expected.

There's no doubt in my mind that you (like me) have said to yourself at one time or another, *"This was NOT the way things were supposed to be."* Maybe your disappointments relate to your marriage, a dating relationship, your job or career, your finances, your health, or a relationship with your parent or child. What I've personally discovered is disappointment, when left unchecked in my life, can often lead to discouragement, which can lead to depression and ultimately despair or apathy– the complete loss of all hope. When our reality does not match the level of our expectations, we experience disappointment. But can I challenge you to rethink your disappointments?

"DISAPPOINTMENT, WHEN LEFT UNCHECKED IN OUR LIVES, OFTEN LEADS TO DISCOURAGEMENT WHICH CAN LEAD TO DEPRESSION AND ULTIMATELY APATHY– THE COMPLETE LOSS OF ALL HOPE."

The enemy of your soul wants you to stay stuck in disappointment so you can downward spiral into despair, become apathetic, and lose all hope in God's good plans and promises for your life and future.

As you encounter various disappointments in life, I challenge you to see your disappointments as divine positioning, not punishment. Choose to see them as destiny in progress rather than destiny denied. See them as divine direction rather than rejection. Too often we see disappointment as a setback when in God's reality, it's a divine setup. And more often than not, there's a divine appointment waiting to meet you in your disappointment.

When you learn to see your disappointments as divinely orchestrated or allowed by God, you can embrace them as opportunities to draw closer to Him and experience His love, grace, provision, and peace in a transformational way.

Disappointment, if we choose to reframe it, is an opportunity to learn more about ourselves–in particular, the perspectives, beliefs and expectations we hold. It's also a great opportunity for us to hear from God and discover *what* and/or *who* we've been placing all our hope and joy in. But may I offer this thought to you? I believe disappointment is an opportunity to shift our thoughts from *"woe is me"* to *"God's got me"* and from *"this is a mess"* to *"this is a divine message."*

There are so many God opportunities awaiting you in your disappointment such as the opportunity to recognize:

- God is able to exceed what you can ask or even imagine *(Ephesians 3:20)*
- God causes all things to work together for your good *(Romans 8:28)*
- God directs your steps *(Psalms 37:23)*
- God delights in every detail of your life *(Psalms 37:23)*
- God promises you a hope and a future *(Jeremiah 29:11)*
- God promises to fulfill His purpose for your life *(Psalms 138:8)*
- God is the author and finisher of your faith *(Hebrews 12:2)*
- God's ways are not your ways; your plans are not His plans *(Isaiah 55:8)*
- God is who you need to place your hope and trust in *(Proverbs 3:5)*
- God's timing and ways are always good and perfect *(Romans 12:2)*

Pictured left and on page 58 is one of my favorite places to walk, explore nature, and engage in bird watching: Martin Park Nature Center, Edmond, OK.

So the next time you feel disappointment rising in your heart, choose to see it as a *divine appointment* —an opportunity to place your trust and hope in God's promises because "such hope (in God's promises) *never* disappoints us, because God's love has been abundantly poured out within our hearts through the Holy Spirit who was given us" (Romans 5:5).

RETHINK:
How would my life (my mental and emotional state) improve if I chose to look for the divine appointment in my disappointments?

_____
_____
_____

REFLECT: What divine opportunities await me in my disappointments?

_____
_____
_____
_____

RESOLVE:
I will see my disappointments as opportunities to receive God's peace, provision, protection and promises.

PRAY:
Father, please forgive me for focusing on the displeasure of my unmet expectations, hopes and dreams. Help me to trust you are directing my steps and working all things out for my good. Lord help me to see my disappointments as opportunities to place my faith, trust and hope in you. Thank you for meeting me in my disappointments, for directing my steps, and for delighting in every detail of my life. I ask these things in Jesus' name, amen.

REMEMBER
Disappointment is a divine opportunity to steep your life in God-initiative and God-provision.

16

Trust God from the bottom of your heart; don't try to figure everything out on your own. Listen for God's voice in everything you do, everywhere you go; he's the one who will keep you on track.

PROVERBS 3: 5-12 MSG

Your decisions direct your destiny

CAN I BE REAL WITH YOU? During the pandemic, I packed on the pounds. Now, the pounds didn't accumulate in a short time period. They slowly accumulated over a few years. But when my husband bought a scale, I finally mustered up the courage to weigh myself IN SECRET–and I was devastated.

I could not believe the number I saw. The last time I saw a number like that was when I was pregnant with my son (who is now a teenager!) Weighing myself was a reality check. It was a defining moment for me. Would I allow the truth to propel me into action or would I allow it to propel me into discouragement and depression? I chose the former.

A defining moment *(or moment of truth as some call it)* is a moment in time where we make a decision that has important consequences on our future. Defining moments have the potential to change the course of our lives. They can increase our health and happiness or decrease it. Defining moments also test our character. Will we decide to persevere and make the necessary changes and sacrifices to achieve our goals *(such as losing weight, getting healthier, getting out of debt, etc.)*? Or will we choose to do nothing, remain the same, or become worse off?

For me, I refused to continue on the unhealthy path I was on. I took action and changed my entire lifestyle by adopting a whole food plant based life style and exercising regularly. If there's something I've learned about change and achieving goals is they both require DISCIPLINE. And discipline demands CONSISTENCY and SACRIFICE. Goals such as losing

Pictured left and on page 64, Garden of the Gods in Colorado Springs, CO (2022). This park is a National Natural Landmark featuring breathtaking sandstone rock formations. I loved this couples trip with my big brother and bonus sister!

When my husband bought a scale, I finally mustered up the courage to weigh myself IN SECRET– and I was devastated.

weight or writing this devotional have required me to sacrifice some things consistently. I've had to say NO to certain foods and sitting on my rear. I've even had to say NO to things I enjoy such as podcasting in order to focus on my health and writing goals.

From a consistency standpoint, I had to commit to writing a certain number of words every day. When it came to getting healthier and losing those extra pounds, I had to commit to exercising 4-5x a week and stick to a whole-food plant-based diet.

But here's the thing about defining moments. They all begin with a decision. And **our decisions** *(when we act on them instead of just talk about them)* **can become turning points in our lives**. What defining moment is facing you right now? What decisions in your life do you need God's wisdom on? Maybe it's a decision related to your marriage, your finances, your friendships, your faith, your career, your mental health, or physical health.

You're only one decision away from determining the direction of your legacy, your future, your marriage, your family, your health, and your wealth. What decision does God want you to make? It will require discipline (consistency + sacrifice) BUT WITH GOD—YOU GOT THIS! I pray you will choose to step into your defining moments by faith and then watch God change the course of your life!

RETHINK:

What do I need to rethink about the quality of my decisions? In what direction are my decisions leading me? Is this the direction God wants?

_____

_____

_____

_____

REFLECT:

What defining moment is facing me right now? What areas of my life do I need to be more disciplined? What areas of my life do I need to submit to God?

_____

_____

_____

_____

RESOLVE:

I will make decisions that please God and direct me to my God-given destiny.

PRAY:

Father, forgive me for making decisions based on my emotions, fears and doubts. Help me to listen for you voice in every decision I make and to trust my steps to you. I know my decisions determine my life direction and destiny. I don't want to avoid hard decisions and end up in destinations you and I never intended. Please give me an understanding and discerning heart so I can make decisions that glorify you and catapult me to my God-given destiny. I ask these things in Jesus' name, amen.

REMEMBER
The quality of your decisions shapes the quality of your life. Decide wisely.

Your
setbacks
are
divine
setups

17

> **"**
> *I have not failed. I have discovered 1000 ways NOT to invent the light bulb."*

This is what Thomas Edison is alleged to have said when asked about his many unsuccessful invention attempts. And yet, we have the invention of the light bulb today because Edison *refused* to quit despite each setback. I'm sure each disappointment along the way was difficult, but he didn't allow it to stop him. Edison didn't view his setbacks or 'failures' as fatal or final; instead, he saw each attempt as an opportunity to learn what worked, and what didn't. How do you view your 'failures' and setbacks? Do you see them fatal or final, or as fuel for success?

When outcomes don't meet our expectations, disappointment can be a natural response. All too often, disappointment sounds like: "This isn't the way it was supposed to be" or "If I only had _____ this _____(insert undesirable outcome) wouldn't have happened."

Two women in the Bible, Mary and Martha, also experienced profound disappointment when Jesus arrived four days after their brother Lazarus had died (John 11:17). They expressed this to Jesus, saying, *"If only you been here, my brother wouldn't have died."* Mary and Martha expected Jesus to stop what he was doing and immediately return to Judea upon hearing that Lazarus was ill. They believed He could have healed Lazarus and prevented his death. But, for reasons unknown to them at the time, he didn't, and allowed Lazarus's death. But not without a greater purpose.

How often do we, too, tend to blame God, our parents, a boss, or friends when things don't turn out as we'd hoped?

In our disappointment, we often say things like "If only my parents would've _____, I'd be better off or more successful." Or "If only my boss or co-worker had

_____

I wouldn't have lost my job" or "If only _____ had shown up and helped me, I wouldn't be in this bad situation." And on, and on we go. Blaming God and people.

Disappointment not only tempts us to blame God or others for our unfavorable outcomes, but it can also lead us to lose hope if left unchecked. How many of us quit on a goal or dream because we were discouraged by the outcome of our efforts? When we don't succeed at something we've worked hard for, it's easy to let disappointment stop us from persevering toward our goal or God-given dream.

Why are we so disillusioned into thinking setbacks and disappointments aren't part of pursuing any meaningful goal? The question isn't *if* we'll face challenges, setbacks, or discouragement — we most certainly will. But *when* we encounter them, do we persevere, or do we give up? Do we look for lessons in our setbacks, or do we look for someone to blame?

Our enemy, Satan, aims to use these setbacks to discourage us from pursuing our God-inspired dreams. He wants us

to doubt God's greatness, goodness, and grace, and use discouragement to shift our focus from trusting in God's purpose, to dwelling on our pain. If disappointment and discouragement take root it our hearts and minds, Satan knows we'll be tempted to fixate on our struggles rather than on God's bigger plans, potentially causing us to miss the divine appointments within our disappointments.

Mary and Martha felt disappointed when Jesus didn't arrive or act in the way they'd hoped. In their disappointment, they even blamed Him. But what they couldn't see was that Jesus had a divine appointment in mind. They didn't realize He was setting up something far greater. Jesus used Lazarus' death and resurrection as an opportunity to reveal His Father's power. He met

Lake Hefner, OKC walk at sunset with my son and husband (2023). Dallas Museum of Art sculpture page 66.

Mary and Martha right in their place of disappointment, appointing a miracle to unfold *after* they faced their greatest sorrow. And He wants to do the same for you, because disappointment often opens the door to receiving a revelation from God.

But we have to choose to look for the divine appointment in our disappointment, for that is where God has arranged to meet us.

Do you believe God wants to meet you in your disappointment? Do you trust He can transform your setbacks into a message, ministry, or miracle—and turn your pain into purpose?

Choose to focus on God's perspective—on what He can do—because His reality can transform any setback or disappointment into a ministry, miracle, or message for your good and for His glory.

RETHINK: What do I need to reframe when it comes to a present or past setback or disappointment that I've been perceiving as fatal or final?

_____

_____

REFLECT: In what ways have I been more attached to my life outcomes than attached to my belief in God's power to set me up for a blessing?

_____

_____

_____

RESOLVE: My disappointments are opportunities to increase my faith and receive a revelation, blessing or miracle from God.

PRAY: *Father, I have allowed disappointment to distract my focus and discourage my heart. Help me to see disappointing life experiences as an opportunity for you to increase my faith and perform a miracle. I don't want to blame you or other people when my reality fails to meet my expectations. I know you will cause ALL things to work together for my good because I love you and I'm called according to your purpose. God, for every disappointment or loss I experience in life, help me to see your hand in it so I can give you the glory for it. I ask this in Jesus's name, amen.*

REMEMBER
Though you can't predict, control or demand a desired outcome for your circumstances, you can know with great certainty that in Christ, disappointment is never fatal or final in light of eternity.

Your
Value

LOOK TO THE CROSS TO KNOW HOW VALUABLE YOU ARE.

YOUR PURPOSE

YOUR PERSPECTIVE

18

You are divinely designed for impact

—

19

Your personality is purpose FULL

—

"God has proved your value by giving His life for you!"

Radhika Cruz

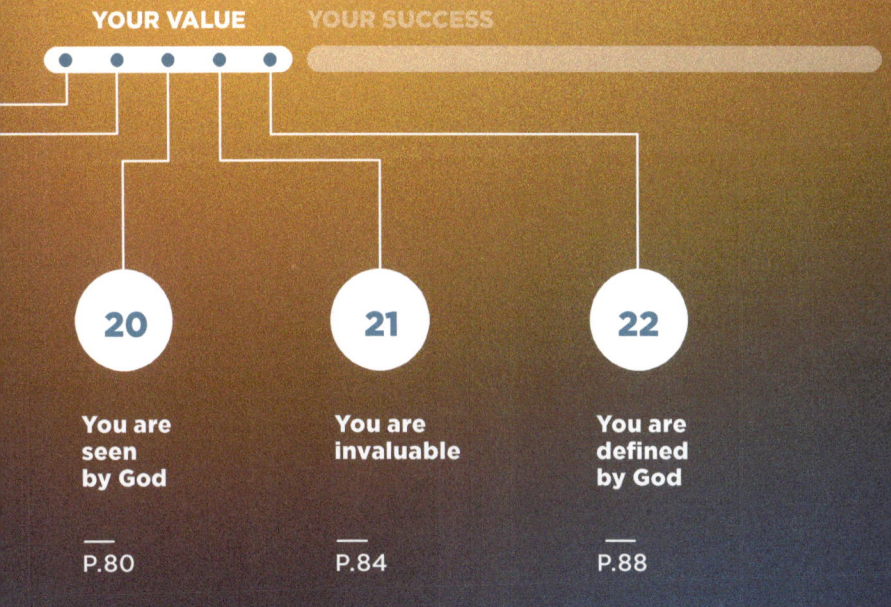

YOUR VALUE   YOUR SUCCESS

20

You are
seen
by God

P.80

21

You are
invaluable

P.84

22

You are
defined
by God

P.88

You are divinely designed for impact

"You're not inspirational."

Words spoken to me by a highly respected and influential leader. To be fully transparent, hearing this caused me, *for a season,* to doubt that I had what it takes to be an impactful leader. After all, aren't leaders supposed to be inspiring?

In all fairness, I don't think this leader meant to harm me, but those words still left a mark. You see, I valued this person's perspective deeply, so much so that I began to question my own value and ability to inspire. But after some weeks of self-doubt and self-loathing, I knew I had a decision to make. I could either agree with this opinion, or I could choose to reject it. I chose to reject it.

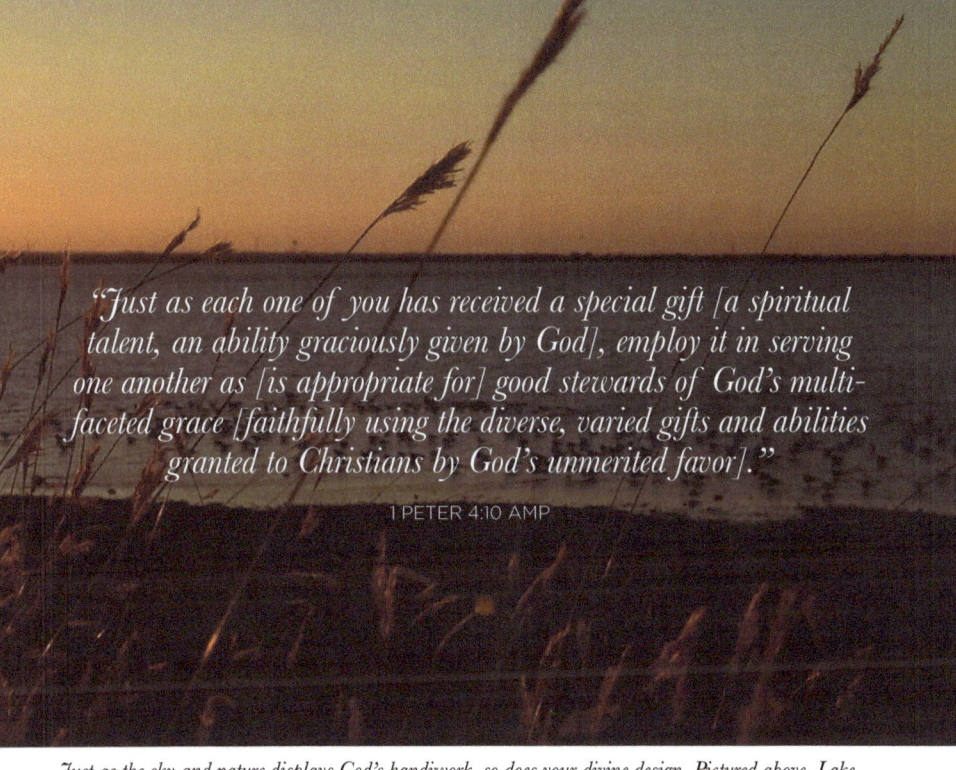

"*Just as each one of you has received a special gift [a spiritual talent, an ability graciously given by God], employ it in serving one another as [is appropriate for] good stewards of God's multi-faceted grace [faithfully using the diverse, varied gifts and abilities granted to Christians by God's unmerited favor].*"

1 PETER 4:10 AMP

Just as the sky and nature displays God's handiwork, so does your divine design. Pictured above, Lake Hefner, OKC.

We often don't realize how our words can take the wind out of someone's sails, causing them to doubt their God-given purpose and potential. To be clear, I hold no hard feelings toward this person; I actually love them dearly. And God, in His goodness, used this experience to help me grow.

How, you might ask? Well. This situation led me to seek the Lord for validation, comfort, and assurance. I learned that sometimes, people will have a limited view of our gifts and potential simply because they don't see us the way God does. People are imperfect and have limited perspectives on the many ways others are gifted to lead, influence, and inspire. And if this leader had understood that there are *countless* ways to inspire others, I doubt they would have spoken those words to me.

But let me tell you. This experience didn't make me bitter; it actually made me *better*. It led me to seek God's perspective on how He has uniquely designed me to inspire and influence others. Friend, if someone has spoken a limiting or negative belief over your potential, abilities, or gifts, I want to encourage you to reject it. You don't have to accept or believe every opinion that comes your way.

But may I challenge you to reflect on this question? **Do you know what God says about you? Do you know the amazing treasures He's placed inside you, even if others can't see, believe, or acknowledge them?** People may not always recognize your giftedness—just look at King David. His own family couldn't see the king in him. Joseph's family couldn't recognize the world-class leader within him.

Pictured above, Old Town San Diego State Historic Park (2018).

And consider Jesus. Many saw Him only as a carpenter, missing the truth that He was the Son of God and Savior of the world.

The reality is, people won't always see or believe in your gifts, purpose, or greatness, and that's okay. What's important is that YOU believe it. You are equipped by God with everything you need to fulfill the assignments He has planned for your life.

Did you know there are 33 distinct attributes statistically linked to inspiring others? Research from Bain[5] shows that you only need one of these 33 traits to be an inspirational leader. When I learned this, I realized I possessed *several* of these traits! And I believe you do, too. Even if others can't see or believe in your gifts, genius, or greatness, YOU MUST SEE IT AND BELIEVE IT—BECAUSE YOU ARE GOD'S MASTERPIECE!

Remember, it doesn't matter what others don't see, say, or believe about you. **What matters most is how God sees you.** So choose to see yourself as He does: gifted, talented, wonderful, and inspirational. See it. Say it. Believe it. And **now go be it**, for the glory of God!

RETHINK: What do I need to rethink when it comes to how God has uniquely designed me to impact the world around me?

_____
_____
_____
_____

REFLECT: What are my inspirational traits and how can I use them to inspire and influence others toward good and godly things?

_____
_____
_____
_____

RESOLVE: I have been uniquely gifted to lead, inspire and influence others because God's inspirational and influential spirit lives in me.

PRAY: _Father, I thank you that the calling you've placed on my life is irrevocable and the gifts you've given me are an expression of your power in action. Please help me to remember I am significant because you have given me a special purpose and function to fulfill in the body of Christ. Lord help me to use the gifts you've given me to do your will and advance your purposes all the days of my life. I ask these things in Jesus' name, amen._

REMEMBER
God has designed and equipped you with everything you need to fulfill the purpose He has for your life.

Your personality is purpose FULL

I praise you because I am fearfully and wonderfully made.

PSALMS 139:14 NIV

Scissortail Park sunflower, OKC, and pictured on page 78, Lily Pond, Botanical Building, Balboa Park, San Diego, CA (2018). I treasure and delight in urban green spaces!

HAVE YOU EVER FELT MISUNDERSTOOD, unaccepted, unwelcome, unwanted, or uncelebrated because of your personality?

A few years ago, someone told me that my personality "got on their nerves." Let's just say that didn't leave me feeling all warm and fuzzy. Instead, their words hurt deeply. Although they later apologized, and I have since forgiven them, I still remember exactly how those words made me feel: misunderstood, rejected, unappreciated, and unwanted. And even though I believe they didn't intend to hurt me, the reality is—they did.

It's ironic, isn't it, how powerful words can be? Sometimes, they can hurt more than sticks and stones. Now, some might argue that words only have the power we give them, but it's undeniable that words shape how we feel and think about ourselves. Just ask the hundreds of thousands of young people in foster care who've been impacted by negative words spoken over them.

But here's what I want you to know, no matter what your personality is like: you are fearfully and wonderfully made in the image of God (Psalm 139:13-14). And guess what? There is NOTHING wrong with you. That's right! You're not a misfit, a weirdo, or somehow defective. Though genetic and environmental factors play a role in shaping our personalities, God can transform our unproductive, unhealthy, or challenging traits to reflect His glory.

Did you know that God often uses our personality weaknesses to help us rely on His strength? We all have weaknesses, but God's Word reminds us that our weakness can be a portal for His power to work in us and through us (2 Corinthians 12:9-10). So instead of feeling defeated by our struggles, we can actually delight in them because it's when we're weak, that He's so strong in us!

THERE IS NOTHING WRONG WITH YOU!

The truth is, we all fall short in various areas of life (Romans 3:23), and none of us have perfect personalities. Each of us has blind spots, and each of us needs a Savior to cover our sins, shortcomings, failures, and faults. But we're all a work in progress, covered by God's grace. And just as God offers us grace for our flaws, we're called to extend grace to others for theirs, too.

But don't ever forget: You are God's handiwork, His masterpiece. He crafted you with a unique personality, specifically designed to fulfill a unique purpose on this earth. So don't you dare let others look down on you, or make you feel "less than" because of the way God designed you. You are not less than desirable, less than wanted, less than loved, less than accepted, or less than valuable. You are enough, just as God intended you to be.

Remember, it was God who formed your inmost being, who knit you together in your mother's womb. And it was God who gave you that distinct mix of traits, qualities, temperament, and tendencies that make you — you. You are one of a kind, gen-u-ine masterpiece.

There's no one else in this world exactly like you. So hold your head up high, with confidence, knowing your personality is divinely designed for a purpose. Therefore, YOU are purpose-FULL!

YOU'VE BEEN DIVINELY DESIGNED
to accomplish God's great purposes

RETHINK: What do I need to rethink or reframe when it comes to my personality?

_____

_____

_____

_____

REFLECT: What can I do to embrace and celebrate my purpose-full personality?

_____

_____

_____

_____

_____

RESOLVE: I will rest assure knowing God's divine power has given me everything I need for life and godliness (2 Peter 1:3).

PRAY: _Father, thank you for making me your one-of-a-kind masterpiece. Help me to stop comparing myself to others so I can start celebrating how you made me. Thank you for being intentional in designing me. Please help me to remember I was made in your likeness with significance and honor which sets me apart as your unique creation in this world. I ask these things in Jesus' name, amen._

REMEMBER

You were made carefully, wonderfully, beautifully and reverently by God. You were not mass produced. You are one of a kind masterpiece.

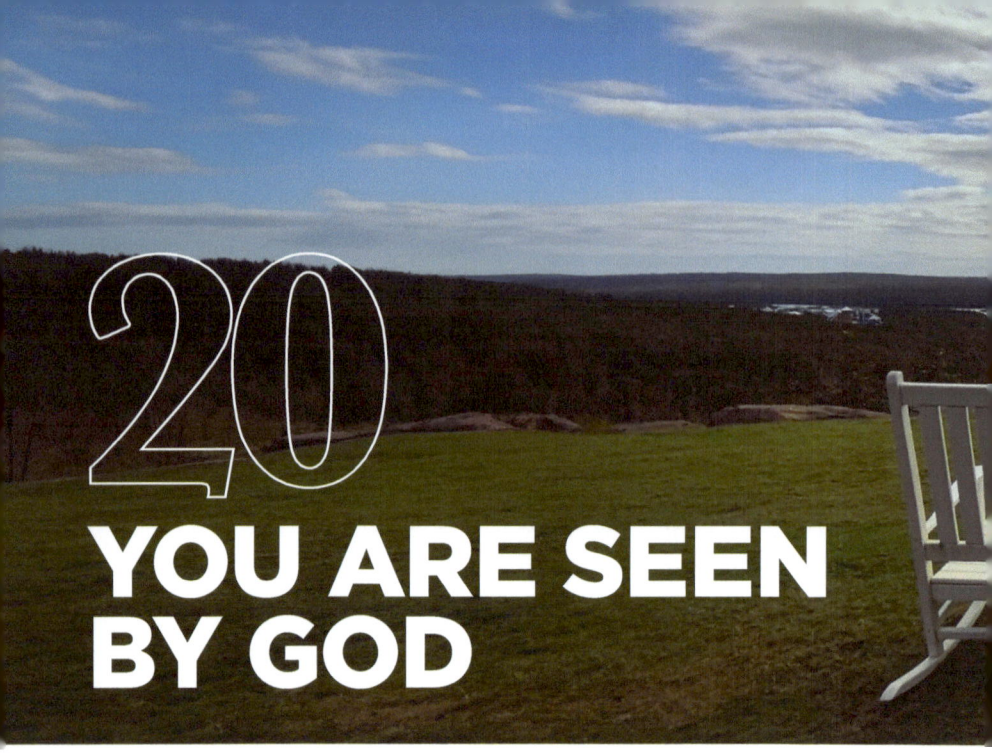

20
YOU ARE SEEN BY GOD

Celebrated my 24th wedding anniversary in 2020 at Carlton Landing, Lake Eufaula, Oklahoma (above).

She gave this name to the Lord who spoke to her: "You are the God who sees me," for she said, "I have now seen the One who sees me."

GENESIS 16:13 NIV

HAVE YOU HEARD THE TERM *SOCIAL invisibility?* It describes groups in society that have been systematically disregarded and marginalized, making people feel insignificant, unseen, or invisible. These "invisibles" are often victims of systemic racism, abuse, discrimination, generational poverty, and trauma.

According to an article in Huffington Post[6], *"invisible people all too often have been deemed by society as "scum."* And I once heard someone say, ***"The only thing worse than being alone is being invisible, because it feels as if you're dead and forgotten by others."***

When I think of the *'invisibles'* in our society, I think of the immigrant and the indigenous. I think of the orphan, children or youth in foster care, and the widow. I think of those experiencing homelessness, the refugee facing a loss of home and culture, and those struggling with infertility or mental health challenges. I think of people with physical, intellectual, or developmental disabilities. I think of people living in the hood *(public housing projects)* and those barely surviving using government assistance. I think you get my point.

The *"invisibles"* include the disadvantaged, the disenfranchised, the disconnected, and the distraught.

If you're reading this and would say to me, *"I can relate to feeling invisible, unseen, or unloved"*, I want you to know that God sees you and cares about you! Even if society looks past you or turns away from you, God turns His face toward you! He knows you by name and is for you. People may forget you, shame you, reject you, laugh at you, or ignore you, but God sees you and He receives you! He is not blind to the pain others have caused you.

Take comfort in the story of Hagar from the Bible (Genesis 16). Hagar was a woman who was treated harshly by another woman in her life, but God heard her cries of distress and sent an angel to encourage her (Genesis 16:9). Just as He responded to Hagar's suffering, **God sees, hears, and will respond to your pain**. He knows who has wronged you, how they made you feel invisible, and how deeply it's hurt you. Friend, you are not forgotten or invisible to God. He sees your tears, hears your cries, and desires to comfort you.

Remember, mistreatment by others doesn't define your worth. Even Jesus, in all of His glory and divine greatness, was not recognized as the son of the only true God. Jesus was also despised, rejected and mistreated by people because they didn't recognize He was God in the flesh, the One sent to save them from their sins! The One who is the way and the truth and the life!

If Jesus faced this, why should you be surprised when you experience the same? Don't allow others' failure to recognize your value make you doubt your significance.

Hold your head high, knowing you are fully loved, fully seen, and fully cherished by God.

Though you may feel invisible to people, you are never invisible to God. And though it may seem like the world is against you, remember God is with you, working all things out for your good. **Your identity, worth, and significance aren't defined by people—they are defined by God.**

As you go to God with your feelings of invisibility, what is He calling you to do?

Just as the angel told Hagar to go back to Sarai and submit to her authority with courage, God may be asking you to release the shame that others' actions have left behind on you. Do you need to ask God to remove your shame-based thinking and help you become rooted and grounded in His unconditional love and acceptance so you will know beyond any shadow of doubt that you are fully seen, known, heard, loved and accepted by God? When you embrace the truth that you're **always** seen and loved unconditionally by God, you'll never feel unseen, invisible, or forgotten again.

RETHINK: What do I need to rethink when I feel rejected, disregarded or invisible to people?

_____

_____

_____

_____

REFLECT: What evidence supports the truth that I am wanted, loved, accepted, celebrated, valued and seen by God?

_____

_____

_____

_____

RESOLVE: I am fully loved, seen, known, and cherished by God.

REMEMBER
You are not invisible or forgotten by God. He sees you. He's for you. He's in it with you and He's fighting for you.

PRAY: _Father I am so thankful to be loved, known and cherished by you. When I feel rejected and invisible to people, help me to remember you see me and you accept me as I am, flaws and all. Thank you for turning your face toward me, being gracious to me, and giving me your peace that surpasses all understanding. I am thankful you know my name and every hair on my head. When I feel unseen, help me to remember I am your child who has been created on purpose to fulfill your great purpose. I ask all this in Jesus' name, amen._

Pictured left, my son attempting the iconic crane kick from the Karate Kid movie at Lake Hefner, OK. He was only 9 years old in this picture!! Time flies!

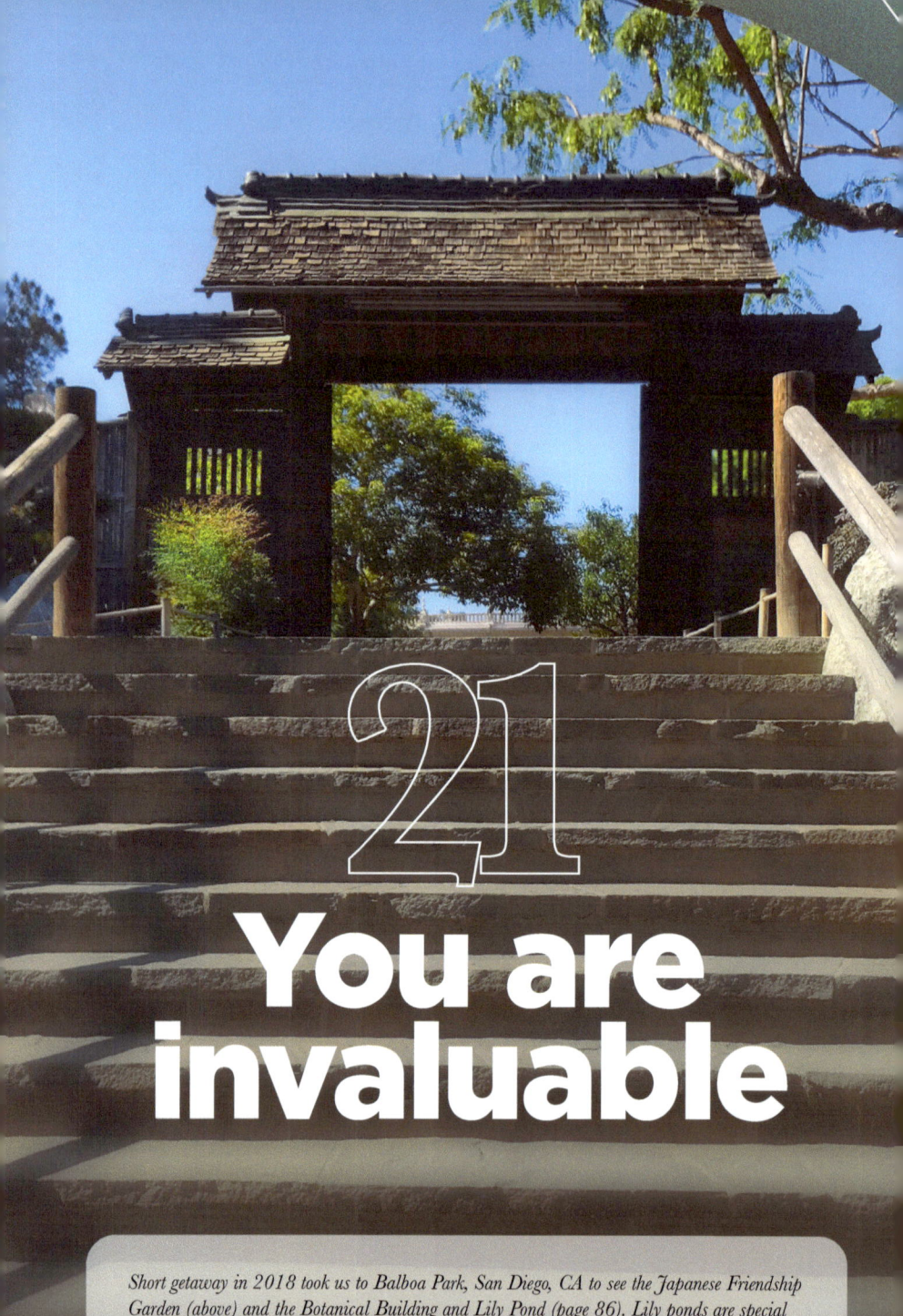

21

You are invaluable

Short getaway in 2018 took us to Balboa Park, San Diego, CA to see the Japanese Friendship Garden (above) and the Botanical Building and Lily Pond (page 86). Lily ponds are special to me because in 1996 I was proposed to at Mill Creek Park's Lily Pond in Youngstown, OH.

When God made you, He said you were "very good"

SOCIAL COMPARISON. IT IS THE thief of joy, gratitude, contentment, and self-acceptance. It's a never-ending measuring stick that deceives us into feeling behind, inferior, inadequate, or lacking. It can make us overlook our own strengths, gifts, and worth, pulling our focus to what we seem to lack instead of what we already have. Social comparison tempts us to measure our value based on how we think we "stack up" against others.

Whether consciously or subconsciously, we compare our personality, profession, possessions, popularity, and parenting against others. We might even compare our appearance, family, relationships, intelligence, talents, and personal achievements too. When we continually compare *who* we are and *what* we have (or don't have) to the highlight reels and success stories of those in our daily lives or on social media, we risk trapping ourselves in a constant state of disappointment, discontentment, and discouragement. And over time, this pattern can lead to thoughts of inadequacy, or feelings of loneliness, frustration, and despair.

The truth is social comparison can lead to low self-esteem, loneliness and depression — if we let it. If God had wanted us to have someone else's gifts, talents, looks, fame, or possessions, He would have given them to us. But He made each of us individually, calling us *"very good"* as we already are (Genesis 1:31). Period.

Social comparison can feel like a vicious cycle where we'll always find ourselves coming up short in some way, shape, form or fashion. And in our efforts to validate our worth, status, or significance, we may find ourselves caught up in people-pleasing, performing, posturing, and self-promoting — all in the hopes of earning the approval, acceptance, and applause of other people. But these behaviors only reinforce the lie that our value comes from outside ourselves, when in truth, our worth is inherent in our identity as children of God.

Sometimes, the desire to compare ourselves to others arises because we don't fully recognize the truth: that we are **already** loved, accepted, worthy, and enough in God's eyes. When we forget whose image we bear, we may be tempted to chase society's standards of success and worth and strive to receive validation from people.

But no societal measure of success, status, or beauty will ever satisfy our deepest need to be loved, valued, and significant. These standards are illusions — counterfeit measures designed to deceive us into believing our success, value, and worth lies in others' approval and acceptance. True validation, however, comes from understanding who we are in God.

I believe our struggles with social comparison often hint at an unmet expectation or hidden disappointment we have with God. We might feel He's held something back from us, that He somehow missed the mark when He created us. We may think, "If only I had their talent, their appearance, or their life, I'd be more successful and valuable." We may even think He's been unkind to us because He chose not to give us *x, y, and z* like so and so, or because He chose not to make us

as attractive, successful, influential, gifted and intelligent like so and so. Now, of course, we'd never express these things out loud to God, or even other people, but if we're being honest with ourselves, many of us carry these hidden beliefs. But here's the game-changer: **When your self-worth is rooted in God's acceptance and approval, you no longer need validation from people.**

When you realize there's no room for comparison or inferiority because you're fearfully and wonderfully made by God, you can finally embrace who you are and find peace in all that God has given you (Psalm 139:14). Remember, you don't have to engage in comparison or impression management through self-promoting to present an image that proves your worth *because you're already valuable to God and your significance has already been placed IN you by God!*

So. Ask God to transform the way you view yourself. Let go of comparing your life to the highlight reels of others. Recognize your worth as a child of God and resist the temptation to seek the approval, validation, and acceptance of people. And make sure you *"Honestly assess your worth by using your God-given faith as the standard of measurement, and then you will see your true value with an appropriate self-esteem"* (Romans 12:3 TPT).

Then, release the need for others' approval or applause to feel valuable. God has already validated your worth. He proved it on the cross. **Rest in the truth that in God's eyes, you are already loved, valued, and worthy—just as you are. Embracing this truth will help you to remember there's not anything you ever need to prove to other people.**

RETHINK: What do I need to rethink when it comes to comparing myself to others?

_____

_____

REFLECT: What unmet emotional need or false belief is driving me to self-promote or seek out the approval, affirmation, validation and applause from people? What truth do I need to believe in order to stop this behavior?

_____

_____

RESOLVE: I will no longer seek approval or validation from people because I know Christ is in me, therefore. I'm loved, valuable, accepted, and enough.

PRAY: *Father, I praise you because I am fearfully and wonderfully made in your image. Please help me to be content with who I am, flaws and all. Help me to be grateful for all the gifts, talents and treasures you've deposited inside of me. Father, I only want to conform to the image of Christ and not the preferences or opinions of other people. I thank you that my identity, value, significance, worth, confidence and acceptance is found in you and not in my performance, personality, talents, abilities or social perceptions of me. Thank you for helping me reject the spirit of comparison so I can fully celebrate my divine design and worth in you. I ask these things in Jesus' name, amen.*

REMEMBER
The evidence of your true worth is found in Christ dying for your sins so you may have eternal life.

See how very much our Father loves us, for he calls us his children, and that is what we are!
1 JOHN 3:1 NLT

22

You are defined by God

ANYONE WHO KNOWS ME WELL KNOWS I LOVE A THOUGHT-provoking or inspirational TED talk. Recently, I listened to a talk by psychotherapist Lori Gottlieb[7] on the subject of self-stories. She shared how the stories we tell ourselves *about ourselves*, can sometimes keep us mentally and emotionally stuck.

She explained that we often assume our circumstances shape our self-stories, when in reality, **it's our self-stories that shape our lives.** That's why they are so powerful. If we can change negative, disempowering, and limiting self-stories into positive, empowering, and victorious ones, we can change our lives. Psychotherapist Ian Morgan Cron expresses it like this: **"Your true self lies beneath the false stories you tell yourself about who you are."** In other words, if the story you're in contradicts who God says you are in HIS story, then you're in the wrong story.

When I think about negative self-stories, I'm reminded of Moses, Gideon, and Jeremiah in the Bible. In Exodus 3-7, Moses repeatedly questioned why God chose him because of his negative self-story. He asked God "Why me?" *"I don't talk well. Look at me. I stutter and stammer. They won't listen to me or trust me. Please send some*one *else!"* Moses pointed out all the reasons he felt inadequate and therefore, pleaded for God to send someone else.

Similarly, Gideon, in Judges 6, was called a **"mighty warrior"** by an angel, yet doubted these words because of his negative self-story saying, *"How and with what could I ever save Israel? Look at me. My clan is the weakest and I'm the runt of the litter."* Jeremiah also felt inferior and inadequate when God told him he was to be His prophet to the nations. Jeremiah's negative self-story was he was too inexperienced, didn't know how to speak, and was too young to do what God was asking of him. (Jeremiah 1:6).

But God's response to each of these men's negative self-stories was incredible. He reminded them of their true identity. He told Moses he would make him like a god to Pharaoh and that he would be heard and trusted as a leader. To Gideon, God called him his mighty warrior and called Jeremiah his prophet, His national spokesperson.

For a long time, I, too, embraced negative self-stories. I told myself I was inadequate, not a leader, not gifted with words, and that no one would want to listen to what I had to say, let alone invest their money to read what I had to say in a book! **Have you ever felt this way?**

Have you doubted your abilities and asked God, "Why me?" Or given excuses for why you couldn't do something, believing you weren't enough? If so, you're not alone. I too have often felt this way and as we see, so did Moses, Gideon and Jeremiah. But over time, I realized I was not living in God's story for me; I was in a self-limiting story of my own making. And I failed to realize who God called and created me to be.

The truth is, **God calls us not as we see ourselves but as He created us to be.** He speaks to us from a place of divine identity, purpose, and power.

Our 25th wedding anniversary getaway in 2021 took us to the Wichita Mountains National Wildlife Refuge pictured above & on pg. 88. This was the first time I saw the Milky Way! It took my breath away!

So often view ourselves through the lens of status, trauma, insecurity, and inadequacy—but God sees us as fully capable, powerful and worthy. God's story for us is one of '**becoming**' and **"God making us into who He called us to be"** rather than a place of us making ourselves.

Contrary to popular belief, we are not "self-made"; we are God-made. God is the one shaping us into who He wants us to be, empowering us to fulfill His purposes. **GOD does the making, calling and the sending —we do the trusting, obeying and depending on God to make us into who He wants us to be.**

Just as He promised to be with Moses, Gideon, and Jeremiah and that He would put HIS words into their mouth, teach them what to say, and direct them on what to do, He will do the same for YOU because whoever He has in mind for you to become—and whatever He has called you to do—you can be it and do it because **He's in it with you, working through you,** and fighting for you! Isn't it encouraging to know that God will give you the strength, guidance, and courage you need to become who He has called you to be?

So. If the story you've been telling yourself is one of limitation, lack, insecurity, inadequacy, inferiority, insignificance, powerlessness, helplessness or incompetence, you're in the wrong story my friend. It's time for you to get into God's story. **It's time to believe who He says you are, so you can accomplish what He's called you to do—not by your own power, but by His Spirit.**

Remember, you are not what you feel about yourself. You are who God says you are: a beloved child, capable, gifted, and equipped through Him to do great works that glorify God. Never let negative self-stories undermine God's power to make you who He has envisioned you to be. Choose to walk by faith and step confidently into God's story for your life because that is where your true purpose and potential lie.

RETHINK: What do I need to rethink concerning who God says I am?

_____

REFLECT: What lies and negative self-stories have been weighing me down and holding me back from doing and becoming all God wants me to do and become? What do I need to do to get into God's story concerning who He says I am and what I can do through Him?

_____

_____

RESOLVE: I accept and embrace who God says I am. A child of God. A friend of God. And an ambassador of God who is more than a conqueror.

PRAY: _Father thank you for opening my eyes to the lies I've believed about who I am and what I thought I was incapable of doing. For every thing I think I'm not, please help me to remember who you say I am. And for everything I think I can't do, help me to remember all I can do through you because with you and through you, all things are possible. Father, help me to no longer entertain self-stories of lack, limitation, inadequacy, insignificance and incompetence. Help me to stay in your story which is one of unlimited power, abundance, security, strength and ability. And for any time in the future that I may doubt my divine identity, power, or potential, Lord please help my unbelief by reminding me of who YOU say I am and what YOU say I can do through you. I ask these things in Jesus' name, amen._

REMEMBER Your identity and value are defined by God alone.

Your Success

GODLY SUCCESS IS BEING TRANSFORMED INTO THE LIKENESS OF GOD.

YOUR PURPOSE

YOUR PERSPECTIVE

23

Success is your obedience to God

24

Success is following God's priorities

25

Success is guarding your heart

26

Success is focusing forward

"What if success wasn't what you achieved but who you become?"

Radhika Cruz

Success
is your
obedience
to God

23

> ❝
>
> *And what do you benefit if you gain
> the whole world but lose your own soul?*
>
> MARK 8:36 NLT

HOW DO YOU DEFINE success? This was the question I asked my son during our bedtime routine when he was 12. Thanks to social conditioning *(insert sarcasm here),* he believed success meant having **a lot** of money. Like my son, so many believe success means acquiring wealth, possessions, popularity, fame, influence, power, and status. For all too many, making a name for oneself is *the ultimate measure* of success. Yet others, *who may feel a more altruistic calling,* see success as making a meaningful contribution to the world and helping *others* succeed.

What if success wasn't something you achieved, but rather someone you became or a child you raised? What if success wasn't found in your *striving* but in your *surrendering* to God? What if success wasn't about influencing the masses, but about influencing *just one* person? And what if true success had little to do with the growth of your accomplishments, and had everything to do with *the growth of your character, freedom, surrender, faith, generosity, and obedience?*

I used to think success meant achieving my dreams and goals—acquiring the dream car, career, partner, money, and home. But after many talks with God, I've learned that success is in my daily obedience to Him. It's in aligning my decisions with His vision for my life. It's about living out my divinely

Pictured above, Pineapple Fountain, symbolic of wealth, luxury and hospitality at Waterfront Park, SC (2023). Pictured left, Charleston Pier, SC.

ordained purpose: to love and serve others, to help build His kingdom, and lead others to Christ.

The Bible tells us that "winning souls is wise" (Proverbs 11:30). So, in God's eyes, winning souls is success because He does not wish for anyone to perish without Him (2 Peter 3:9).

Pictured above, Face Fragments sculpture in Edmond, OK by Susan Evans (photo taken in 2023).

This is why He sent His Son—to be our Savior, so that by faith, we will be saved from the wages of sin, which is death and eternal separation from God.

So you see, **godly success isn't about you**—your wealth, status, or influence. However, if God has blessed you with these gifts, He's done so to bring Him glory and to serve **His** purposes, which *always* involves loving people and the winning of souls. Godly success is being fully committed to loving God and others well, living in obedience to His Word, and teaching others to do the same. "For what does it profit a man to gain the whole world and lose his soul?" (Mark 8:35).

I don't want to achieve success by the world's standards. For what good is it for me to gain all of my heart's desires, yet forfeit my own soul? I want godly success, which means obeying God and winning souls (Proverbs 11:30). **How about you?**

96

RETHINK: What do I need to rethink or reframe in terms of being successful?

_____

_____

_____

_____

REFLECT: In what ways have I allowed the world to influence my idea of success? What godly success metrics do I need to live by? _____

_____

_____

_____

_____

RESOLVE: I will define my success by God's standards and not the world's standards.

PRAY: _Father, thank you for helping me see that success is about my obedience to your will, ways and word. Help me to forsake the world's standards for success and adopt your standards which includes loving, obeying and serving you —and loving, serving and leading people to you. I ask these things in Jesus' name, amen._

REMEMBER
Success is your obedience to God and seeking to fulfill His vision and purpose for your life.

24 Success is following God's priorities

HAVE YOU EVER SAID SOMETHING WAS A PRIORITY FOR YOU BUT when you looked at your actions, there was a discrepancy? I know I have. I've always said my physical health and fitness were important, but my actions told a different story. I wasn't scheduling routine check-ups with my doctor or dentist, and I certainly wasn't exercising regularly. The truth is, if something is truly a priority, we make time for it. Period. Priorities are simply deeply held values and convictions that we act upon.

All too often, we say our faith, finances, or fitness are priorities, but our actions reveal otherwise. As I just stated, if something is important to us, if we truly value it, we make the time for it.

So, how do we know if our priorities are aligned with our values? To answer this, we must explore what we genuinely believe is important in life. Do you know what your core values are? If I asked, *"What's most important to you in life?"* how would you respond? Or, **if you died today, what one thing would you be most disappointed in not completing, achieving or fulfilling?**

Why is it that we so often prioritize the urgent—*the things with clear deadlines and immediate consequences*—over the truly important things that lead to a meaningful and fulfilling life in the long run? Taking time to align our actions with our true values is what

If something is truly important to us, if we truly value it, we make time for it.

Pictured left, Crystal Bridges Museum of American Art, Bentonville, AK (2019). Pictured on page 101, Dallas, Texas Arboretum and Botanical Garden (2016). I love art museums and botanical gardens! So much beauty to discover!

turns priorities into reality. Far too often, we hold *idealistic* priorities—values we declare in our words but rarely in our deeds. We have good intentions, but lack follow-through. If we want to be truly value-driven, even purpose-driven, *we must discern what genuinely matters from what does not.* And knowing this requires us to take an honest look at what we believe is most important in life.

So. Imagine yourself at the end of your life, taking your last breaths. What regrets would you have? If we want to live a life with minimal regret, we must identify what matters most to God and direct our focus and actions on *those* things. This means clearing out *everything* that distracts us from what *God values most.*

So often, we prioritize status, fame, wealth, and possessions, but are those truly God's priorities? While God may give us these things to glorify Him and fulfill His purposes, what He values most is the saving of souls—the salvation of the world.

The truth is our achievements, our character, and the impact we have in the world are reflections of what we choose to focus on. Ultimately, these are outward signs of what we believe matters most in life.

And in reality, we're all going to end up somewhere in life. Don't you want to end up living in God's purpose — a life rich with meaning and free of regret? It's not too late! You can choose to start NOW!

We are all going to end up somewhere in life. Don't you want to end up in God's purpose?

RETHINK: What do I need to rethink when it comes to what matters most in life?

_____

_____

REFLECT: In what ways have I been living misaligned from God's priorities?

_____

_____

RESOLVE: I will align my values and priorities to God's vision, values and priorities and focus my attention and actions on those things.

PRAY: _Father, thank you for helping me to be intentional in living a life with fewer regrets. Help me to steward this life you've given me with a strong sense of meaning, purpose and mission. Please help me to stay focused and aligned to your vision, goals and priorities for my life. Lord forgive me for all the times I've focused on the wrong things. Help me to focus my attention and efforts on the things that matter most to you. I ask all this in Jesus' name, amen._

> ### REMEMBER
> When you align your values, goals and priorities to God's vision, values and priorities, you will live a purposeful and meaningful life with no regrets.

> *Guard your heart above all else, for it determines the course of your life.*
>
> PROVERBS 4:23 NLT

Success is guarding your heart

ONE THING I'VE ALWAYS avoided in life is scary movies and TV shows. Growing up in the '80s, I remember a sci-fi television series called *"The V"*. In this show, a humanoid, lizard-like extraterrestrial race came to Earth, and blended into society with a hidden agenda: steal the planet's water, control its population, and harvest humans for food.

In full transparency, that show terrified me as a kid, filling me with a fear that has stuck with me. Since then, I've never enjoyed watching shows or movies that evoke fear. As a parent, I've learned I must be mindful of what I allow my children to watch or listen to because I understand how media affects our hearts—our mind, will, and emotions. Therefore, guarding their hearts, and my own, feels essential.

When you guard your heart, it means you're intentional about what you allow to shape your thoughts, beliefs, values, attitude, behavior and life. The truth

is, what we feed our hearts and minds regularly shapes our mindsets, habits, and attitudes—and ultimately, our destiny—for good or for bad, for better or for worse.

The enemy of your soul will often use people, social media, movies, television shows, and music to influence your heart away from God. After all, Satan's aim is to destroy your character, purpose, joy, peace, integrity, purity, and influence. We can not be ignorant of his devices. We must remain vigilant, discerning the influence of these things and stay anchored in God's word. We must **guard our hearts above all else, for it determines the course of our lives** (Proverbs 4:23).

Guarding your heart requires courage, especially when faced with everything that tries to pull you away from God. Do whatever is necessary to guard your heart against things that could ensnare you and harm your mind, character, influence, and purpose. If that means unfollowing

---

Pictured left, "Remnant Heart", Condensed water color and black marker illustration by my daughter, Janae Cruz. (2015). This illustration represents the one heart and soul we've been given that continues to flourish and grow throughout our life journey on earth.

accounts on social media—UNFOLLOW. If it means deleting social media altogether—DELETE IT. If it means abandoning certain television shows, music, or places, go ahead and follow through with it. With God's help, I've done this and so can you!

Please don't let culture, social pressure, or FOMO *(fear of missing out)* convince you to hold on to people or habits that aren't building you up in faith, character, and purpose. There's too much at stake, and there's no time to waste.

"Therefore, since we are surrounded by such a huge crowd of witnesses to the life of faith, let us strip off every weight that slows us down, especially the sin that so easily trips us up. And let us run with endurance the race God has set before us" (Hebrews 12:1).

WHEN IT COMES TO GUARDING YOUR HEART, THERE'S SO MUCH AT STAKE AND THERE'S NO TIME TO WASTE.

Pictured left and on page 105, Eisenhower State Park, Lake Texoma (2016). This was the year we relocated to Oklahoma from Maryland and on this family trip we explored caves, swam, and visited Amazing Jake's in Plano, TX.

RETHINK: What do I need to rethink when it comes to what I'm allowing into my eyes, ears, mind and heart?

_____

_____

REFLECT: Which people, places and practices do I need to abstain from in an effort to guard my heart?

_____

_____

RESOLVE: I refuse to conform to the patterns of this world. I choose to guard my heart and renew my mind by washing it with God's word daily.

PRAY: *Father, I recognize the course of my life is determined by the condition of my heart—my mind, will and emotions. Please give me the power to resist anything and everything that seeks to turn my heart against your will and ways. Please forgive me for failing to give careful thought to the corrupt people, places, paths and practices that have caused me to think and act in ways that are not pleasing to you. Help me to be aware of the snares, devices, schemes and intentions of the enemy so Satan can not deceive me and have an advantage over me. Lord, create in me a clean heart and renew a right spirit within me. I thank you that my heart can be transformed and made righteous by your Spirit as I meditate on your Word/Truth day and night. Father, I ask these things in Jesus' name, amen.*

REMEMBER
You guard your heart, your life source, through righteous living which is the standard God requires.

Success is
Focusing Forward

IT'S OFTEN SAID THAT for every ending there is a new beginning. When we begin something new—a job, a career, or even a new year—we tend to set goals. Fitness goals, financial goals, relationship goals, career goals. But the Apostle Paul had a higher goal: a heavenly one. His focus was on eternal life, a forward focus toward what God had called him to. In Philippians 3:13-14, Paul urges us to pursue the same goal with relentless passion and reckless abandon.

If we want to become and do all that God has purposed for us to do,

Pictured above, Lake Hefner, Oklahoma City. This reservoir was built in the 1940s to expand the water supply for Oklahoma City. Did you know that Oklahoma City is the 8th largest city in the Southern United States? Pictured on page 108, Scissortail Park, OKC and on page 109, Wheeler Park Ferris Wheel, OKC.

we must to stop focusing on what's behind us. To receive what He has for us, we have to stop looking back at our past, the *"good old days."* And this isn't always easy, is it? Especially when the past holds meaningful and joyful memories.

Years ago, I left behind some close friends, a vibrant, diverse city, and a church family that truly enriched my life. After our family relocated to Oklahoma, I found myself continuously looking back at my past—longing for the life and people we left behind. But on one particular day, while I was driving in my car, God clearly spoke to my heart, saying:

"Don't look back. Look forward to the future I have for you" (Genesis 19:17). This word reminded me of Genesis 19, where Lot's family was told to not look back as they left the city of Sodom. But Lot's wife disobeyed, and this attachment to her past cost her dearly. Because the moment she looked back, was the moment she died. Her desire for what was behind was stronger than her desire to look forward to the future God planned to give her.

When we don't understand why God closes a chapter we loved, or a relationship, job, or season we thought would last, it's tempting to hold on to those things because we fear for our future. We worry and wonder, "What's next for me? Will the new thing in my future be as good as or better than what I had?" I know this feeling all too well.

But God showed me that He wanted me to trust my endings, my beginnings, and my future to Him. He wanted me to trust in His promise to prosper me and give me a good future (Jeremiah 29:11). He wanted me to trust that what was ahead of me was greater than what was behind me (Job 42:12). And He wanted me to stop looking back on past seasons so I could look forward to my future with hope, peace, joy and excitement.

Friend. I don't know what you're grieving, longing for, or clinging to from your past, but I know God wants you to stop looking back at what once was. He wants you to look forward to your future with hope, joy, and a heart full of great expectancy. God has more good in store for you (Proverbs 4:25; Hebrews 12:1-2). And He wants you to trust that your latter days will be even greater than your former days.

"God wants you to trust your endings, beginnings and future to Him."

And He wants you to fix your eyes on the new things He's doing in your life today (Isaiah 43:19). As you read this, I pray you will start looking forward to your future with a heart FULL of hope and anticipation for all the good that is yet to come to your way. So. Choose to embrace your new beginnings with joyful expectation knowing God's plan to prosper you is already in play!

RETHINK: What thoughts do I need to change about my future to ensure they are thoughts full of hope and joyful expectation?

_____

_____

REFLECT: What do I need to stop longing for OR looking back at in my past? In what areas of my life does God want me to have an attitude of hope and expectation for all the good things yet to come my way?

_____

_____

RESOLVE: I will look to my future with joyful expectation for all the good God has in store for me.

PRAY: _Father I am thankful that you hold my future in your hands and that you have plans to prosper me. Please help me to look to my future with hope and joyful expectation. Help me to remember that you have already ordered my steps and that you delight in every detail of my life. Lord I thank you for your promise to cause me to flourish in every area of my life and in every season of my life, as I stay rooted and anchored in you. I ask all this in Jesus' name, amen._

REMEMBER
God has plans to prosper you, to give you hope and a good future.

Success Requires
Gazelle Focus

*And let us run with perseverance
the race marked out for us,
fixing our eyes on Jesus...*

HEBREWS 12:1 NIV

HAVE YOU EVER HEARD the phrase *"gazelle intensity"* or *"gazelle focus"* popularized by financial advisor Dave Ramsey? Dave describes gazelle intensity as the speed and determination we should bring to creating a spending plan and paying off debt. It's about running from debt as if your life depends on it!

Dave coined "gazelle intensity" from Proverbs 6:1–7, which says, *"If you've signed surety, my son, do this: give no sleep to your eyelids, no slumber to your eyes, and deliver yourself like a gazelle from the hand of the hunter, a bird from the hand of the fowler."*

Dave explains, *"the way you get out of debt is you run like you are a gazelle with a cheetah chasing you. You go crazy. I mean crazy. Intense! So gazelle intense it's as if you're about to be eaten. You run! When you do that and you have that kind of intensity in getting out of debt, you can break the gravitational pull of stupid and move yourself in a better direction. That's what gazelle intensity is—running for your life."*[8]

This "gazelle intensity" has been my new approach as I focus on building stronger family bonds, and greater physical, spiritual, and financial fitness. If you've ever tried to get in shape, you know it takes daily discipline, focus, and perseverance. But since my energy and capacity for gazelle focus is limited, I've chosen to apply it to a few yet most important areas

Pictured left, Martin Park Nature Center. Pictured above, plant life from Balboa Park Botanical Garden, San Diego, CA (2018). I just love succulents and flowers! Don't you?

of my life: my faith, family, finances, and fitness (or health). So what does this look like practically?

From a faith perspective, it means prioritizing daily time with God through prayer and Bible reading. This also looks like my husband and I reading through the Bible in a year using the YouVersion plan, sharing notes and reflections together. For our children, "gazelle focus" in the area of faith-training looks like talking about God in daily life, reading His word together, and going through discipleship materials together. Financially, gazelle focus is living within a strict budget, working steadily to pay off debt (using Ramsey's debt snowball strategy), and giving above our tithe.

All of these priorities require an intentional investment of time, effort, discipline, consistency, and focus. And to give these areas my best, I've made hard choices and sacrifices. I've had to say "no" to some good things—like blogging and podcasting—for a season, so I can give my full attention to my relationship with God, my family, finances, and health. Living with gazelle focus not only requires discipline and sacrifice, but also a clear understanding of what is most important to God and most beneficial to you.

The reality is, our time is non-renewable, making it our most precious resource. Once it's gone, we can't get it back. We can't control time—slow it down, speed it up, or create more of it. The truth is we all have the same 24 hours in a day. The big question is *"What are you doing with the limited time God has given you?"*

Are you using your time to focus on the things of God? Are you maximizing each day to invest in activities that impact your eternity and that of others? Or are you squandering your time, living distracted rather than gazelle-focused? Are you drifting aimlessly and mindlessly without a clear sense of purpose or direction?

We all have limited time on this planet. Know why you're here *(your God-given purpose)* and what you're meant to do *(your God-given mission)*. Live with gazelle focus on your mission and purpose, because one day, when your life is over, you'll stand before God and give an account of how you used the time He gave you. When I stand before the judgment seat of God, I want to hear,

Pictured above, plant life from Balboa Park Botanical Garden, San Diego, CA (2018).

"Well done, my faithful servant! You have been a good steward of the time, talents, and treasure I gave you. Now enter into the joy of your Master" (Matthew 25:23).

Don't you want to hear and receive the same? To do so, you must live with gazelle focus as you discover and live out God's vision, purpose, and mission for your life. Stay focused on these things, no matter the cost, so you can one day enter into the joy and reward of your Heavenly Father for all eternity!

RETHINK: What do I need to rethink when it comes to what I've been focusing my attention and energy on?

_____

_____

_____

REFLECT: What area of my life does God want me to work at with gazelle intensity? What are some of the things I need to stop doing so I can focus more on the things that matter most to God?

_____

_____

_____

_____

RESOLVE: I will live with gazelle focus in the following areas of my life:

_____

_____

_____

_____

_____

PRAY: _Lord thank you making me aware of the urgency, focus and intensity I need to have in order to redeem the time you've given me to do your will. Please help me to be aware of Satan's devices and schemes so I am not overtaken, distracted, deceived, and taken advantage of. Father help me to throw off everything that tries to hinder me from obeying you, pleasing you and doing your will. Help me to run the race you've given me with perseverance and gazelle intensity. I ask all these things in Jesus' name, amen._

> **REMEMBER**
> Living with gazelle intensity requires discipline, focus, perseverance and dependence on God.

Success Is Cultivating God-Confidence

DON'T BE SO NAIVE AND SELF-CONFIDENT. YOU'RE NOT EXEMPT.
YOU COULD FALL FLAT ON YOUR FACE AS EASILY AS ANYONE ELSE.

Forget about self-confidence; it's useless.
Cultivate God-confidence.

1 CORINTHIANS 10:12 MSG

IF YOU HAD ASKED ME 20 YEARS ago what the secret to a successful life was, I would have said something like hard work, determination, persistence, discipline, flexibility, optimism, and risk-taking. But now, with a little more life experience and *(hopefully)* wisdom, I'd answer that question very differently.

When we think about success, many of us tend to see it as a product of our own initiative, effort, or hustle. Webster's dictionary defines success as *"a person or thing that achieves desired aims or attains prosperity, wealth, and fame."*

For highly driven achievers like me, it's easy to rely on my personal efforts, talents, and strengths to achieve what the world defines as success. And although a goal without a plan and action is wishful thinking, God's children need to understand how He defines success.

According to our culture, success is when we reach a prominent position of power or accumulate possessions, wealth, notoriety, popularity, prestige, influence, and admiration.

From this standpoint, success is about self-initiative, self-confidence, and storing up treasures (and appearances) here on earth. But this constant "striving" to get ahead, or achieve success, isn't how God works.

> **Unfortunately, too many people place all their confidence in themselves— their gifts and talents, efforts, economic status, connections, position and possessions.**

1 Corinthians 10:12 (The Message) reminds us: *"Don't be so naive and self-confident. You're not exempt. You could fall flat on your face as easily as anyone else. Forget about self-confidence; it's useless. Cultivate God-confidence."*

Before this verse, Paul reminded the Corinthian church of their history—of how it was God who led their ancestors out of slavery in Egypt and miraculously parted the Red Sea so they could escape on dry ground. He warned them to not repeat their ancestors' mistakes — being overconfident in themselves and placing other things above God.

Unfortunately, many people place all of their confidence in their talents, efforts, economic status, connections, positions, and possessions. But God doesn't want us saying, "My own power has rescued me" (Judges 7:2). He doesn't want us placing confidence in our selves to save our selves. He wants us to put our trust and confidence in Him. God-confidence means trusting in God to be our:

GOD-CONFIDENCE MEANS TRUSTING IN GOD TO BE OUR:

PROVIDER: He supplies ALL of our needs (Gen. 22:13-14; Ps. 23:1)

HELPER: He is our refuge & ever-present help in times of need and trouble (Ex. 17:8-15)

STRENGTH: He gives us the ability to endure/overcome life's challenges (2 Cor. 12:8-10)

COMFORTER: He comforts us in our distress, sorrow and pain (2 Cor. 1:4)

HEALER: He cleanses us from every sickness and disease (Ex. 15:26)

PEACE: He calms all our worries, fears and distress (Jn. 14:27)

DEFENDER: He protects us from enemy attack (Ps. 62:5-7)

SAVIOR: He saves us and rescues us from death (Ps. 68:20)

God-confidence is placing all our hope and trust in God, knowing He has better days ahead for us. And this hope, or God-confidence, is what brings us joy and peace that surpasses all our understanding.

When we place our confidence in God instead of ourselves, we can rest assured He'll show up in our lives and work all things together for our good. Our culture may tell us we're "self-made," that our success comes solely from our own hands. But this is a lie. Every talent, blessing, provision, and gift—whether material or spiritual like love, joy, and peace—ultimately comes from God (James 1:17).

So the next time you're tempted to rely exclusively on your talents, connections, or anything else for success, remember that it is God who ultimately brings you success as you obey and seek Him first.

As someone who is trying to cease striving, may I encourage you with this paraphrased scripture found in Luke 12:29-32?

Relax. Don't be so preoccupied with getting, so you can respond to God's giving. Steep yourself in God-reality, God-initiative, and God-provisions. You'll find all your everyday human concerns will be met. Don't be afraid of missing out because your Heavenly Father wants to give you the very kingdom itself.

RETHINK: What would it look like for me to cultivate or increase my God-confidence?

_____

_____

_____

_____

_____

REFLECT: In what ways have I been so preoccupied with getting? How can I better respond to what God is doing and giving me right now?

_____

_____

_____

_____

_____

RESOLVE: I will cultivate God-confidence over self-confidence.

PRAY: _Father, I thank you that my success in life is rooted in your provision and initiative working on my behalf. Help me to see that a successful life is a surrendered life that hopes in and depends on your love, your goodness, your grace, your provision and your initiative on my behalf. Father help me to depend on your abilities and power to do the things you've called me to do. And please help me to remember that Biblical success is serving you, obeying you, following you and being known and loved by you. I place all of my hope and confidence in you as the One who gives me success and supplies me with everything I need for life and godliness. I ask all these things in Jesus' name, amen._

REMEMBER
Placing all your hope and confidence in God is the true path to experiencing a success-full life.

29
Success is Freedom in Christ

My daughter celebrating our arrival to Magic Kingdom for the "The World's Most Magical Celebration" in 2022. It was Disney World's 50th anniversary and our first time visiting as a family.

D O YOU WANT TO LIVE A LIFE FULL OF SUCCESS? WE ALL DO, right? But maybe a better question is this: **Do you want success as defined by the world or as defined by God**? Here's how I distinguish worldly success from godly success:

- Worldly success focuses on personal wins, while godly success centers on serving others so they, too, can win.

- Worldly success may leave an imprint on society, but godly success always leaves an imprint on someone's eternity.

- Worldly success is often driven by ego or self-importance, whereas godly success is driven by kingdom importance.

- Worldly success seeks to increase our personal value, but godly success aims to add value to others.

Here's another thought for you to consider: What if you measured success by the level of your freedom instead of by worldly standards? Imagine freedom from selfishness, comparison, perfectionism, self-criticism, self-condemnation, and self-loathing. Imagine freedom from poor self-esteem, poor self-image, and feelings of inadequacy. Imagine freedom from addiction and freedom from sin. What if...

◉ What if you experienced freedom from inadequacy based thinking such as "I'm not qualified enough, smart enough, talented enough, or good enough" to "Because I am loved, chosen and unconditionally accepted by God, I am enough."

◉ What if you experienced freedom from impression management where you are no longer consumed with thoughts of "What will people think or say about me?" to "I know what God thinks about me and it's all good."

◉ What if you experienced freedom from regret-based thinking such as "I wish I would've ____" to "I can't change my past but I can make better decisions moving forward with God's help."

◉ What if you experienced freedom from limiting beliefs such as "I'm not ____, I don't ____, I can't ____" to God-empowered beliefs such as "If God is for me, who can be against me?" and "I can do all things through Christ who strengthens me."

◉ What if you experienced freedom from blaming others for how your life has turned? Shifting from "It's my boss's fault I can't get a promotion" or "It's my spouse's fault we're not thriving" to taking responsibility for your life's outcomes and asking God for wisdom?

Imagine how being free from anger, fear, anxiety, worry, depression, doubt, unforgiveness, and jealousy could transform your life. How would it change the way you see yourself, love yourself, relate to, and love others? How would taking responsibility for your life instead of blaming others in your life, impact your present and future "success"? How would this shift affect your mental and emotional well-being, especially if you feel mentally or emotionally stuck?

What if I told you true success is freedom in Christ, in being rooted in His unending, unconditional love and acceptance of you? The truth is the more Jesus is alive in you, the freer you become. So, let's turn away from the world's standards of success—defined by possessions, achievements, popularity, and socio-economic status. Instead, let's embrace a godly view of success, which is being full of the presence of God.

Friend, God doesn't want you enslaved to anything but Him— not to sin, food, work, hobbies, video games, TV, alcohol, pornography, or drugs. We are called to serve nothing but Jesus, the One who is "the way, the truth, and the life" (John 14:6).

REMEMBER: A truly *successful* life starts with a *surrendered* life to Jesus. And a surrendered life to Jesus leads to a *holy* life — a life *free from the bondage of sin* which results in *eternal life with God.*

Pictured above, and on page 121, our family explored the Tulsa Botanic Garden after attending the Oklahoma Comic Con and Global Gathering event at the Gathering Place in Tulsa, OK (2024). I so treasure these family experiences together. They are truly priceless!

RETHINK: How have I been striving to achieve success by the world's standards? What do I need to rethink as it relates to success?

_____

_____

REFLECT: What sin, beliefs, blame game, mindsets or spiritual strongholds are stopping me from walking in freedom? What steps do I need to take to be set free?

_____

_____

_____

RESOLVE: I choose to be a slave of God, which is the only true freedom.

PRAY: *Father, I don't want to gain worldly success and forfeit my soul and eternal dwelling place. Please forgive me for measuring my success and significance by the world's standards because true success is my freedom which is found in being full of Jesus. Help me to die to my sin and flesh daily so I can pick up my cross and follow you. Help me to remember I was bought with a price, and that my life is not my own. Lord I acknowledge I belong to you. Please help me to submit myself to you so I can do your will all the days of my life. I only want to be a slave to you God. Thank you for setting me free. I ask these things in Jesus' name, amen.*

REMEMBER
True freedom is found when you become a slave of God.

Success is Being Rooted in Christ

DID YOU KNOW THAT PLANTS can communicate with each other? It's true! Before the world wide web existed, the *wood wide web* existed! Researchers have discovered a "*wood wide web*"[9] that allows trees in a forest *(such as Birch and Fir trees)* to communicate with each other, and share water, nutrients and minerals to each other by way of their vast root network. Older established "mother trees" known for having their roots established in deeper soil, send vital resources, like deep water and nutrients to support younger saplings or distressed trees.

It is this remarkable *mycorrhizal*[10] network that not only helps trees survive but also strengthens the health and resilience of the entire forest ecosystem. Strong and deep root systems are essential for plant well-being and survival. Take for example the famous wild fig tree in Echo Caves South Africa[11]. The root system (or taproot) of this tree measures almost 400 feet deep[12], making it the most deeply rooted tree in the world. Taproots are also found in plants such as dandelions, radishes, carrots, beets and trees such as oak, pine and fir. A taproot's main purpose is to provide deep anchorage to the tree and aid it in absorbing nutrients and water from the soil. Plants that have a deep root system are very strong, drought tolerant, and resilient.

Figuratively speaking, taproots are thought of as the source of an idea, work, or in some cases, the source of one's inspiration or strength. It's a proven fact deep roots are the source of a plant's strength. And you know what? This fact also holds true for those who are deeply rooted in Christ.

"LET YOUR ROOTS GROW DOWN INTO HIM,
AND LET YOUR LIVES BE BUILT ON HIM.

Then your faith will grow strong in the truth you were taught, and you will overflow with thankfulness."

COLOSSIANS 2:7 NLT

When I learned about the "wood wide web" and heard about the taproot system of this wild fig tree in South Africa, I was reminded of Colossians 2:7-8 that says:

"And now, just as you accepted Christ Jesus as your Lord, you must continue to follow him. Let your roots grow down in him, and let your lives be built on him. Then your faith will grow strong in the truth you were taught, and you will overflow with thankfulness. Don't let anyone capture you with empty philosophies and high-sounding nonsense that come from human thinking and from the spiritual powers of this world, rather than from Christ."

As we can see, God desires for our roots to grow deep in Him so that we may grow strong in faith and not be swayed by human logic, empty philosophies, or false doctrines.

When we accept Christ as our personal Lord and Savior, we are choosing to live for His glory and pleasure, rather than our own and choosing to honor God with our entire lives—our mind, body, spirit, and actions. Furthermore, as we allow God to transform, lead, and use us, our lives become firmly established *(or built) on Him.*

But our roots cannot grow deeply in God until we **surrender completely**, giving Him control over our thoughts, actions, and entire lives. If we allow worldly beliefs, values, philosophies, and teachings to capture our attention, they can deceive our hearts and corrupt our thinking, hindering our growth in faith and godly character.

Letting our roots grow deep in Christ involves three key practices:

1. **Paying close attention to God's Word:** We should crave and obey it, and allow it to guide our lives.

2. **Gathering with other believers:** We persist in prayer, rejoice at all times, give thanks to God in every circumstance, and extend love, grace, and forgiveness to everyone.

3. **Staying sober-minded and self-controlled:** We must put on the full armor of God and remain alert and vigilant against the snares and attacks of the enemy.

By doing these things above, we can stand strong, resist the enemy, and remain firm in our faith. In the end, we will receive the crown of life—God's reward for loving Him, serving Him, and remaining steadfast amid our trials, tests, and temptations. Our strength and stability depends on being deeply rooted in Christ, which comes through obeying His Word and submitting to His Spirit's leading.

Just as taproots are the source of strength to plants, Christ is the source of **your** strength. When you are anchored in Christ— through His Word and Spirit, and remain in the habits of prayer, worship,

Pictured on page 122 is the 145 ft. Tree of Life from Disney World's Animal Kingdom. Pictured above is the Valley of Mo'ara from Pandora—The World of Avatar. This was our second time visiting Disney World (2023) and Pandora did not disappoint! With its exotic plants, enormous floating mountains and glowing fauna and flora, it was truly breathtaking and other worldly! What a magnificent display of nature and a testament to the power of our imagination!

and fellowship with other believers—you will gain the protection, strength, security, stability, hope, and grace needed to grow, flourish, and produce rich fruit for the Lord. You will also be able to endure the trials and storms of life without being uprooted (losing your faith and hope, or giving in to sin).

If you want to receive the crown of life, it's essential to persevere through temptations, trials, tribulations, persecution, and challenges with unwavering faith. But the key to your strength is being deeply rooted in Christ — His love, Word and Spirit.

If you're reading this, it's not too late to let your roots grow deep in Him. All it takes is a simple invitation: Invite Jesus to be your personal Lord and Savior. Acknowledge with sincerity that you believe He is Lord and that He died for your sins. Next, confess your sins, faults, and shortcomings to God. Ask Him to forgive you and cleanse you from all unrighteousness. Ask Him to transform your thinking, fill you with His Spirit, and make you aware of the enemy's schemes so you won't be taken advantage of. Seek to know and understand God's good, pleasing, and perfect will for your life so you can embrace it wholeheartedly.

Ask Him to renew your mind, helping you break free from worldly patterns of thinking. Remember, God is for you, not against you (Romans 8:31). Nothing you've done or will do in the future can separate you from His love—not your fears, worries, nor any power in hell (Romans 8:31-38).

If you have yet to fully surrender your life to Christ, I urge you to do so right now. The Bible tells us that our lives are but a vapor—here one moment and gone the next (James 4:14). Tomorrow is not promised to you. But because God loves you immensely, He sent His one and only Son so that if you believe in Him, you will not perish but have eternal life. Throughout life, you will face many decisions that shape your *earthly* destiny. But no decision compares to your decision of being deeply rooted in Christ, because this decision affects your *eternal* destiny. *Today,* God is offering you a choice: between life and prosperity, or death and destruction (Deuteronomy 30:15). You can choose to be grounded in Christ or in the world. You can choose to build your life on Christ, or on yourself.

I pray you choose to *deeply root* yourself in Christ and **build your life on Him**, for Jesus is the only true way to eternal life and glory with our Heavenly Father (John 14:6). Friend, choose to build your life on Christ and watch your life be **richly blessed!**

RETHINK:
What would it look like to let my roots grow deep in God?

_____

REFLECT:
What empty philosophies or ungodly thinking have I allowed to capture my attention and deceive my heart (my mind, will and emotions)?

_____

_____

RESOLVE:
I will build my life on God by developing an intimate relationship with Jesus.

PRAY: *Father, thank you for reminding me that building my life on anything other than Jesus is sinking sand. Please help me to guard my heart so I don't allow ungodly and secular thinking capture my attention and deceive my heart. Help me to anchor my life in the habits of daily prayer, studying your Word, worshiping in your house, and gathering with other believers. Please renew my mind as I meditate on your Word and make me more aware of Satan's schemes so I won't be deceived, taken advantage of, or sin against you. Lord, I want my life and faith to be built on Jesus so I can please you and receive the crown of life as my reward. I ask all this in Jesus' name, amen.*

REMEMBER
When you build your life on Christ, your life will be blessed.

Acknowledgments

Johnny. Thirty-one years together. Twenty-eight years married. Two children together and two significant losses too. You are my best and closest friend, my chief encourager, cheerleader and life-coach. You are my favorite person in the entire world and God's greatest gift to me. You love me unconditionally, serve me sacrificially and enthusiastically, and build me up daily. You are the wind beneath my wings, my sunshine on a cloudy day, and the best wingman a wife could ever have. Thank you for always using your creative gifts and graphic design talents to bring my projects to life. This book would not exist without your creative genius, constant support, and relentless love. Team Cruz baby all the way, every day, until death do us part! Te amo!

Dad. I would not be who I am today without you. Your love for reading inspired my love for reading which in turn, inspired my love for writing. Thank you for helping me obtain my very first library card, regularly taking me to the library and bookmobile, and always buying me Scholastic books when I was in elementary school. It was my childhood dream to be a writer when I grew up so here I am! Thank you for being an amazing listener, patient teacher, loving father, encouraging friend, and godly example for me to follow. You are one of God's best gifts to me and I am so thankful God gave me you as a father and close friend.

Mom. Although you are no longer with me in the flesh, your spirit lives on in me and in your grandchildren. And although I'm not able to give you a signed copy of this book, I want you to know you were a significant driving force behind it. When you transitioned to glory in 2008, I longed to know more of your God-story and your perspective on various life issues. And it was because of this longing I decided to capture some of my very own God-stories to pass down to my children so they could have a tangible record of things God has taught me, brought me through, and revealed to me in my own faith walk. Thank you for always praying for me. Thank you for never giving up on me, especially when I ran away and went astray. And thank you for introducing me to the greatest love of all. Jesus.

My Champion and Cruz family. **Rob**. My first and longest best friend. Thank you for always encouraging me to persist toward any goal I set, especially when I want to quit. And thank you for being one of my biggest supporters and cheerleaders. I thank God for choosing you to be my big brother. My life is richer and fuller because you're in it. To my other siblings, Cai, Chrissy, Alicia, and Josh— and to my bonus siblings, and bonus parents Juan and Maria, thank you for loving me and accepting me just as I am. I love each and everyone one of you and pray this book blesses your life and children tremendously!

You. Thank you for trusting me to speak into your life and encourage your heart with this book. Please know my perspectives and divine revelations are only meant to be used as resource for you, not a conclusion. In order for you to gain the most insight and revelation on all of life matters, you must seek God through prayer and the reading of His Word, and allow His Spirit to guide you into all truth. I pray these reflections and revelations give you the encouragement you need to restore or increase your peace, joy and hope, reframe your disappointments, bounce back from your setbacks, and understand your true value and God-given purpose so you can achieve godly success—a life characterized by a wholehearted love for God, obedience to God, submission to God, freedom in God, and unwavering confidence in God so you can be directed and empowered by God to become and do every single thing He's planned for you to do and become. May you always remember that God, your Creator, has created you on purpose, for a specific purpose. May you remember God is still writing your story and He has so much MORE in store for you! More than you could ever ask or imagine. Just you wait!! Just you wait!!

About the Author

Radhika Cruz is a wife of 28 years, mother of two, and sister to five siblings. She has served in vocational ministry as a marriage and family life director, children's ministry director, and community group director at two different multicultural megachurches in the U.S. (Maryland and Oklahoma). She also served as a worship and band director for 8 years at a multicultural, bilingual (Spanish-English) church in Youngstown, Ohio.

Radhika is an American author *(this is her first published book)*, faith-based blogger and podcaster who published forty-four podcast episodes and approximately one hundred blog posts during the global pandemic. She has digitally published a *Career Thrive Guide* to support professional flourishing, a *Godly Girl's Guide to Getting Unstuck* to help women overcome their limiting beliefs, and *Mindset Reset*, a guide for how to overcome destructive mindsets and disempowering self-talk.

In her leisure, Radhika enjoys traveling, watching movies with her family, hiking in nature, visiting botanical gardens across the U.S., exploring local bookstores and coffee shops, visiting art museums, and attending fine and performing arts events (of which *Hamilton*, *In the Heights* and *Wicked* are her favorites)! She is a Pittsburgh, PA native (technically from McKees Rocks) who currently lives in Oklahoma City, Oklahoma with her husband and two children.

Website: www.radhikacruz.com
Podcast: Lead Love Thrive!
Instagram: @madeformoredevo
LinkedIn: linkedin.com/in/radhika-cruz

When she's not enjoying her family or outside exploring nature, you can find her serving in her home church or operating in her professional capacity writing workforce development curriculum, designing and facilitating adult learning events, or hosting statewide conferences and leadership development events for Oklahoma human services executives and professionals. No matter her role, her mission is to help others rise to their potential, live out their purpose, and do GOOD things with GREAT love for the glory of God.

Notes

4: You are perfectly designed for your purpose.

1   https://www.freeshapetest.com/

7: Your divine disruptions.

2   Feiler, Bruce. (2020). *Life is in the transitions.* Penguin Random House.

8: Your Perspective Matters

3   Burnham, E.S. (2017, February 20). Finding my purpose in prison. *Adopt an inmate.* https://adoptaninmate.org/finding-purpose-prison-eric-burnham/

13: Placing your hope in God anchors your life.

4   Gwinn, C., & Hellman, C. (2022). *Hope Rising: How the science of hope can change your life.* New York, New York: Morgan James Publishing.

18: You are divinely designed for impact.

5   Horwitch, M., & Callahan, M. W. (2016, June 09). How leaders inspire: Cracking the code. *Bain & Company.* https://www.bain.com/insights/how-leaders-inspire-cracking-the-code/

20: You are seen by God.

6   McCarthy, M.J. (2017, December 06). Society's invisible people. *Huffpost.* https://www.huffpost.com/entry/societys-invisible-people_b_849731

22: You are defined by God.

7   Gottlieb, L. (2019, September). How changing your story can change your life. *TED.* https://www.ted.com/talks/lori_gottlieb_how_changing_your_story_can_change_your_life

27: Success requires gazelle focus.

8   Ramsey, D. (2018, June 10). *Facebook.* https://www.facebook.com/daveramsey/posts/you-might-have-heard-the-term-gazelle-intense-before-but-have-you-ever-wondered-/10155616436380886/

30: Success is being rooted.

9   Holewinski, B. Underground networking: The amazing connections beneath your feet. *National Forest Foundation.* https://www.nationalforests.org/blog/underground-mycorrhizal-network

10   Simard, S. (2016, June). How trees talk to each other. *TED.* https://www.ted.com/talks/suzanne_simard_how_trees_talk_to_each_other

11   Greatest root depth. *Guinness World Records.* https://www.guinnessworldrecords.com/world-records/66407-greatest-root-depth

12   Deepest Roots. *Damooga Foundation.* http://damoogafoundation.org/about_trees.php

RAAF Captures
Flying Saucer
on Ranch in
Roswell Region!

The flying object landed on a ranch near Roswell sometime last week. Not having phone facilities, the rancher stored the disc until such time as he was able to contact the sheriff's office, who in turn notified Maj. Jesse A. Marcel of the 509th Bomb Group Intelligence Office.

Action was immediately taken and the disc was picked up at the rancher's home. It was inspected at the Roswell Army Air Field and subsequently loaned by Major Marcel to higher headquarters.

—*Roswell Daily Record,* July 8, 1947

Find out
what really happened in
Uncanny Encounters:
Roswell